This
Day *in*
Christian
History

This Day *in* Christian History

WILLIAM D. BLAKE

BARBOUR
PUBLISHING

© 2011 by Barbour Publishing, Inc.

ISBN 978-1-60260-646-3

Published by Barbour Publishing, Inc., P.O. Box 719, Uhrichsville, Ohio 44683, www.barbourbooks.com

Our mission is to publish and distribute inspirational products offering exceptional value and biblical encouragement to the masses.

Member of the
Evangelical Christian
Publishers Association

Printed in the United States of America.

THE WIDE, WONDERFUL WORLD OF CHRISTIAN HISTORY

Through two thousand years, in just about every nation on earth, "Christian history" has been unfolding.

It's natural to think of the faith in terms most familiar to ourselves, in the context of our own time, our own communities, and our own worship styles. But the God who created our large, diverse world has worked through time in ways and places that might amaze us, if only we knew.

That's what *This Day in Christian History* is all about—showing how God has moved in people, nations, and events over the past two millennia, working out His plans for humanity. Through preachers and politicians, missionaries and mothers, books, denominations, hymns, and inventions, the gospel of Jesus Christ has gone forward and changed lives.

Every day for an entire year, you'll find a highlight of Christian history for that particular date, as well as a secondary item—often the birth or death record of a notable figure. By the end of 365 days, you'll have a much larger view of the ways God and humankind have worked to advance the kingdom of heaven on this earth.

1901

Historians trace the beginning of modern Pentecostalism to Bethel Bible School in Topeka, Kansas, operated by former Methodist preacher Charles F. Parham (1873–1929). There, at about 7:00 p.m. on the first day of the twentieth century, student Agnes Ozman begins speaking in tongues.

1484

Birth of Swiss reformer Ulrich Zwingli, whose sermons criticizing the Catholic Mass started the Reformation in Switzerland.

1921

The first religious radio program in U.S. broadcast history is heard when Calvary Episcopal Church of Pittsburgh airs its worship service over local station KDKA. The preacher is the Reverend Edwin Jan Van Etten.

1868

Scottish clergyman and biographer Andrew Bonar writes in his diary, "Lord, this year may the Spirit fill my soul, revealing the fullness of Christ to me from day to day."

1956

The Colored Methodist Episcopal Church officially changes its name to the Christian Methodist Episcopal Church. The denomination originated in 1870, when the Methodist Episcopal Church, South, approved the request of its black membership for the formation of a separate ecclesiastical body. Headquartered today in Memphis, the CME Church has a membership of about half a million.

1816

Birth of Ann Ayres, founder of the Sisterhood of the Holy Communion—the first U.S. Episcopal sisterhood. Ayres was thus the first woman in the United States to become a Protestant sister.

1840

A group of Yale Congregational students opens Illinois College in Jacksonville. The first denominational seminary established in Illinois inspires the rapid spread of Congregationalism in the state.

1581

Birth of James Ussher, Anglican prelate. Ussher published a biblical chronology that dates the Creation to 4004 BC.

1964

Pope Paul VI and Athenagoras I, ecumenical patriarch of Constantinople, meet in Jerusalem. It's the first meeting between Roman Catholic and Greek Orthodox prelates since 1439.

1527

Martyrdom of Felix Manz, twenty-nine, Swiss Anabaptist reformer. Manz is drowned as punishment for preaching adult baptism, becoming the first Protestant martyred by other Protestants.

1924

In England the first worship service broadcast over radio from a church is aired by the British Broadcasting Company. The service is conducted by H. R. L. Sheppard at St. Martin-in-the-Fields Church.

1740

Birth of John Fawcett, English Baptist preacher and poet. More than 160 of Fawcett's hymns are published during his lifetime, including "Blest Be the Tie That Binds" and "Lord, Dismiss Us with Thy Blessing."

367

Athanasius, the early Church father famous for his battles against the Arian heresy, writes a letter containing a list of what he regards as the authoritative books of the New Testament. Over time his list is adopted as the canon by the Church at large.

1844

Birth of Bernadette Soubirous, French Roman Catholic visionary. In 1858, at age fourteen, she experiences eighteen visions of the Virgin Mary in a grotto at Lourdes. Canonized in 1933, she is the subject of the Oscar-winning 1943 film *Song of Bernadette*.

1198

Italian cardinal Lotario de Conti de Segni is elected pope. His reign, as Pope Innocent III, is the most powerful papacy in the Middle Ages and marks the climax of medieval Catholicism. Pope Innocent is the first to adopt the title "Vicar of Christ." His support of the Fourth Crusade results in the capture of Constantinople and the establishment of the Latin Empire.

1956

Death of five American missionaries—Jim Elliot, Nate Saint, Roger Youderian, Ed McCully, and Pete Fleming—killed by the Auca Indians of Ecuador, whom they were attempting to evangelize.

1943

The popular World War II song "Praise the Lord and Pass the Ammunition!" reaches number one on the pop music charts. Performed by Kay Kyser, the song was inspired by the attack on Pearl Harbor on December 7, 1941.

1777

Circuit rider and Methodist bishop Francis Asbury confides in his journal, "My soul lives constantly as in the presence of God, and enjoys much of His divine favor. His love is better than life!"

1984

The United States and the Vatican reestablish full diplomatic relations after severing them in 1867.

1863

Death of Lyman Beecher, American Congregational clergyman, educator, social reformer, and adamant abolitionist. Beecher fathered thirteen children (including Henry Ward Beecher and Harriet Beecher Stowe). All nine of his sons became ministers after him.

1791

The First Day (or Sunday School) Society
is organized in Philadelphia, making it
the first interdenominational Sunday
school organization in America. In 1824
the group merged with others to form the
American Sunday School Union.

1843

Death of Francis Scott Key, Maryland-born lawyer,
poet, and author of America's national anthem.
Key was also among the organizers of the Domestic
and Foreign Missionary Society, founded in 1820.

1972

The South Dakota Episcopal Diocese consecrates the Reverend Harold S. Jones as a suffragan bishop. Jones, a Sioux, becomes the first Native American bishop in the Episcopal Church.

1839

Scottish pastor Robert Murray McCheyne observes in a letter to another pastor, "It is not the tempest, nor the earthquake, nor the fire, but the still small voice of the Spirit that carries on the glorious work of saving souls."

1501

Christianity's first vernacular hymnal is printed in Prague. It contains eighty-nine hymns in the Czech language.

1836

Birth of Alexander Whyte, Scottish clergyman known as "the last of the Puritans." Whyte taught New Testament at New College, Edinburgh, and authored a number of devotional books.

1604

In England the Hampton Court Conference begins, at which Puritan representatives meet with their new king, James I, to discuss proposed changes in the Church of England.

1875

Birth of Albert Schweitzer, French (Alsatian) theologian, music scholar, physician, and medical missionary. His *Quest of the Historical Jesus* (1906) is considered a foundational work in that subject. In 1913 he founded Lambarene Hospital in French Equatorial Africa; and in 1953 he was awarded the Nobel Peace Prize.

1535

The Act of Supremacy is passed, in which King Henry VIII declares himself "Protector and Only Supreme Head of the Church and Clergy of England." (Henry had broken with the Roman Catholic Church. Clement VII voided the annulment of his marriage to Catherine of Aragón and excommunicated him.)

1832

Birth of Susannah (Thompson) Spurgeon, wife of Charles Spurgeon. Susannah began a ministry enabling students of Spurgeon's Pastors' College to buy their needed textbooks.

1604

At the Hampton Court Conference in London, Puritan John Rainolds suggests to King James I "that there might bee a newe translation of the Bible, as consonant as can be to the original Hebrew and Greek." James grants his approval, and the ensuing project leads to the 1611 publication of the Authorized (King James) Version of the Bible.

1819

Birth of Johannes Rebmann, German explorer and missionary to East Africa. Rebmann translated the Gospel of Luke into one of the native languages and helped prepare dictionaries for three African dialects.

1970

John M. Burgess is installed as bishop of the Protestant Episcopal diocese of Massachusetts, making him the first African-American bishop to head an Episcopal diocese in America.

1829

Birth of Catherine (Mumford) Booth, English reformer and wife of William Booth, founder of the Salvation Army. Called "mother of the Salvation Army," Catherine Booth was instrumental in introducing the organization into the United States, Australia, Europe, India, and Japan.

1891

The first Armenian church in the United States is consecrated in Worcester, Massachusetts. In 1898 an encyclical of Catholicos Mugurditch I establishes the Diocese of the Armenian Church of America, and by the beginning of the twentieth century, the Armenian community in the United States numbers more than fifteen thousand.

1815

Birth of German theologian and textual scholar L. F. Konstantin von Tischendorf, who is remembered in scholarly circles for discovering and deciphering the *Codex Sinaiticus*, an important fifth-century Greek manuscript of the Pauline epistles.

1563

The Heidelberg Catechism is published in the palatinate in southwest Germany where the holy Roman emperor resides. Composed by Peter Ursinus and Caspar Olevianus, the catechism comprises a statement of Calvinist tradition designed to unify conflicting Protestant ideologies. Accepted by nearly all of the Reformed churches in Europe, it is still in use in some Dutch and German Reformed churches.

1798

Birth of Samuel Austin Worcester, American Congregational missionary to the Cherokee Indians in Georgia and Arkansas.

1891

Dr. Charles A. Briggs delivers an address at Union Theological Seminary in New York City titled "The Authority of the Scriptures," resulting in a heresy trial. Briggs was eventually found guilty and was defrocked by his denomination's general assembly.

1669

Birth of Susannah (Annesley) Wesley, wife of clergyman Samuel Wesley and mother of nineteen children, including John and Charles Wesley, the founders of Methodism.

1525

At a secret (and illegal) gathering of six men in Zurich, Switzerland, Conrad Grebel (a former protégé of Ulrich Zwingli) rebaptizes George Blaurock, a former monk. This meeting is considered the birth of the German Anabaptist movement.

1886

Death of Laura Maria Sheldon Wright, American missionary to the Seneca Indians in western New York. Her work influenced the establishment of the Thomas Asylum for Orphan and Destitute Indian Children (later the Thomas Indian School).

1899

Pope Leo XIII publishes the apostolic letter "Testem benevolentiae." Addressed to James Gibbons, cardinal archbishop of Baltimore, the letter is remembered primarily for the Vatican's condemnation of "Americanism"—the adaptation of Roman Catholic doctrine to the more independent ideologies of modern civilization, represented primarily by American character.

1588

Birth of John Winthrop in England. He later served twelve terms (1629–48) as the first governor of the Massachusetts Bay Colony and helped to banish Anne Hutchinson for alleged heresy.

1955

The United Presbyterian Church U.S.A. formally approves the ordination of women as clergy, making it the first mainline Protestant denomination to do so.

1777

Anglican evangelical Henry Venn writes in a letter to his son, "A family fearing God, working righteousness, obtaining promises, living in peace and love, is a picture of Heaven in miniature."

1989

The Reverend Barbara C. Harris
of Boston is confirmed as the first
female bishop in the history of the
Church of England.

1573

Birth of John Donne, renowned English metaphysical poet
and dean of St. Paul's Church, London (1621–24). Donne
is known for such memorable lines as "Death be not
proud"; "No man is an island"; and "Send not to know for
whom the bell tolls. It tolls for thee."

1944

Anglican Bishop R. O. Hall ordains Florence Tim-Oi Li as a priest at Shie Hing in Kwangtung Province, China. Lee's ordination was an emergency wartime measure, owing to the lack of male priests in Macao. In 1946 the Diocesan Synod of Hong Kong and South China endorsed the action, thereby making Florence Tim-Oi Lee the first female Anglican clergyperson.

1949

Death of Peter Marshall, Scottish-born American Presbyterian minister. He pastored New York Avenue Presbyterian Church in Washington DC (1937–49) and served as U.S. Senate chaplain (1947–49).

1776

The Reverend Louis Eustace Lotbinière becomes the first chaplain of the American Continental Army when he is appointed to the regiment of Colonel James Livingston by General Benedict Arnold.

1905

Birth of Maria Augusta von Trapp, Austrian-American musician, who fled Nazi-occupied Austria in the 1930s and formed the world-famous Trapp Family Singers. Her story is the subject of the award-winning 1965 film *The Sound of Music*.

417

Pelagius, a British monk whose teachings are declared heretical, is excommunicated by Pope Innocent I. Pelagius's doctrine denies original sin and teaches that one could become righteous by the exercise of free will.

1842

Scottish pastor Robert Murray McCheyne exhorts in a letter, "Call upon the name of the Lord. Your time may be short, God only knows. The longest lifetime is short enough. It is all that is given you to be converted in. They are the happiest who are brought soonest to the bosom of Jesus."

1916

In Washington DC Louis Brandeis is appointed to the U.S. Supreme Court. He is the first Jewish associate justice.

1822

Birth of William D. Longstaff, English philanthropist and hymn writer, who authored the hymn "Take Time to Be Holy."

1972

The historic separation of white and black Methodist conferences in South Carolina ends when the two bodies meet together for the first time and vote to accept a plan of union.

1499

Birth of Katherine von Bora, the former German nun who married Martin Luther. Born into a noble family, Katherine became a Cistercian nun in 1515 but ran away from the convent in 1523 and married Luther in 1525.

1536

Parish priest Menno Simons leaves the Catholic Church over his doubts about transubstantiation. He converts to the Anabaptist faith and leads a group of followers who eventually come to be called Mennonites.

1813

Birth of Samuel P. Tregelles, English Presbyterian Bible scholar who conceived of a new critical text of the New Testament to replace the *Textus Receptus*. The results of his research were published as *An Account of the Printed Text of the Greek New Testament* (1870).

1911

In North Carolina the Fire-Baptized Holiness Church and the Pentecostal Holiness Church officially merge. Four years later, the Tabernacle Pentecostal Church also joined the merger. In 1975 the name of this united body officially became the International Pentecostal Holiness Church.

1949

American missionary Jim Elliot concludes in his journal, "One does not surrender a life in an instant—that which is lifelong can only be surrendered in a lifetime."

1750

Anglican clergyman and hymn writer John Newton marries Mary Catlett. Their marriage lasts forty years, until Mary's death in 1790. John Newton, author of the hymn "Amazing Grace," died in 1807.

1909

Birth of George Beverly Shea, Canadian-born music evangelist, who sang at many of the Billy Graham Crusades from the 1950s through the 1970s.

1881

The first formal church youth organization is established in the Williston Congregational Church in Portland, Maine, by the Reverend Francis E. Clark. Originally called Christian Endeavor, it becomes the forerunner of denominational youth fellowships in modern churches.

1881

American Quaker holiness author Hannah Whitall Smith writes in a letter, "Slowness of movement is no disadvantage in the more advanced stages of spiritual growth.... God is always slow when He is doing a deep and lasting work."

1985

In South Africa Desmond Tutu becomes Johannesburg's first black Anglican bishop. A trained ecumenist, Tutu later becomes archbishop of Cape Town and Anglican primate of South Africa.

1832

Birth of William H. Doane, American Baptist hymn writer and editor of *Sabbath School Gems* (1862) and *The Baptist Hymnal* (1886). Doane also composed the hymns "To God Be the Glory," "Precious Name," I Am Thine," "More Love to Thee," "Near the Cross," and "Rescue."

1874

English poet and devotional writer
Frances Ridley Havergal pens the words
to the popular hymn of commitment
"Take My Life and Let It Be."

1906

Birth of Dietrich Bonhoeffer, German Lutheran
pastor and theologian. A secret member of the
German resistance movement during World War II,
Bonhoeffer was arrested by the Gestapo in April
1943 and later hanged at the Flossenbürg concentration
camp. Bonhoeffer's best-known writings are *The
Cost of Discipleship* (1948), *Ethics* (1950), and
Letters and Papers from Prison (1953).

1631

English-born clergyman Roger Williams arrives in America. He soon begins questioning Massachusetts' religious policies that fuse church and state matters. Banished to Rhode Island five years later, he established the first Baptist church in America in Providence.

1705

Death of Philipp Jakob Spener, German Lutheran churchman and founder of Pietism. Spener introduced reforms in church discipline, use of the catechism, and the training of youth, and his methods became the foundation of confirmation. Spener's *Pia Desideria* (1675) encourages private devotions among serious Christian believers.

1924

Radio station KFSG (Kall Four Square Gospel) goes on the air. One of the earliest licensed radio stations, KFSG broadcasts the services of Angelus Temple, the flagship congregation of the International Foursquare Gospel Church, founded in 1923 by Aimee Semple McPherson.

1931

American missionary and literacy pioneer Frank Laubach writes in a letter, "There is a deep peace that grows out of...loneliness and a sense of failure. God cannot get close when everything is delightful. He seems to need these darker hours, these empty-hearted hours, to mean the most to people."

1528

The Swiss canton of Bern officially embraces the Protestant faith of reformers Ulrich Zwingli and John Oecolampadius.

1832

Birth of Hannah Whitall Smith, American Quaker evangelist, reformer, holiness evangelist, and speaker. Her most influential publication, *The Christian's Secret of a Happy Life* (1875), remains a popular devotional guide to this day.

1693

The College of William and Mary is founded in Williamsburg, Virginia, for the purpose of educating Anglican clergymen. It is the second-oldest institution of higher learning in America, after Harvard.

1936

Death of James Henry Fillmore, Ohio-born clergyman, singing schoolteacher, and sacred music publisher. He wrote and published many cantatas, anthems, and hymn tunes, including "Resolution" ("I Am Resolved No Longer to Linger") and "Hannah" ("I Know That My Redeemer Liveth").

1812

Pioneer missionary Samuel Newell marries fellow Congregationalist Harriet Atwood. They afterward sailed for India with Adoniram and Ann Judson. Harriet Newell and Ann Judson became the first American women commissioned for missionary work abroad.

1914

Birth of Bruce Manning Metzger, American Presbyterian New Testament scholar. Metzger taught at Princeton University (1938–1984) and was a member of the Revised Standard Version Bible translation committee.

1929

In London renowned Baptist
clergyman and devotional author
F. B. Meyer preaches his last sermon.
He died on March 28.

1859

Birth of Jonathan Goforth, Canadian Presbyterian
missionary to Honan and Changte, China. Goforth was
noted for training native evangelists and preachers.

1790

The Society of Friends (Quakers)
presents a petition to the American
Congress calling for the abolition
of slavery.

1948

U.S. Senate Chaplain Peter Marshall prays, "We ask
Thee not for tasks more suited to our strength,
but for strength more suited to our tasks."

1948

The Pentecostal awakening known as the "Latter Rain Movement" traces its origin to this date, when students at the Sharon Orphanage and Schools in North Battleford, Saskatchewan, Canada, begin experiencing a mass spiritual awakening.

1644

Birth of Jacob Ammann, Mennonite minister from Alsace/Switzerland and founder of the Amish Mennonites.

1936

The Lutheran Church–Missouri Synod organizes the Lutheran Army and Navy Commission for the purpose of commissioning chaplains for military service overseas. In 1947 the organization changed its name to the Armed Services Commission.

1919

Birth of Ernest Jennings "Tennessee Ernie" Ford, Christian country entertainer. Ford hosted his own television program (1955–65) but is best remembered for the many sacred musical recordings he made during his career.

1985

The U.S. Rabbinical Assembly of Conservative Judaism announces its decision to begin accepting women as rabbis.

1760

Birth of Richard Allen, the first African-American ordained in the Methodist Episcopal Church (1799), and founder of the African Methodist Episcopal (AME) Church.

1386

King Jagiello of Lithuania is baptized into the Christian faith. Lithuania was the last heathen nation in Europe; thus, Jagiello's conversion became the final fulfillment of the Macedonian vision in Acts 16:9, which led the apostle Paul to begin taking the gospel to Europe.

1905

Death of Lewis Wallace, American Civil War soldier and author of *Ben-Hur: A Tale of the Christ* (1880), *The Boyhood of Christ* (1888), and *Lew Wallace: An Autobiography* (1906).

1865

English clergyman Sabine Baring-Gould publishes "Now the Day Is Over," a hymn based on the text of Proverbs 3:24: "When thou liest down, thou shalt not be afraid. . .and thy sleep shall be sweet."

1809

Former U.S. president John Adams writes in a letter to Judge F. A. Van der Kemp, "The Hebrews have done more to civilize men than any other nation. . . . [God] ordered the Jews to preserve and propagate to all mankind the doctrine of a supreme, intelligent, wise, almighty sovereign of the universe. . .the great essential principle of morality, and consequently all civilization."

.   1889

Billy Sunday, baseball player turned
preacher, makes his first appearance
as an evangelist in Chicago. Sunday
preaches Fundamentalism, supports
temperance, and opposes scientific
evolution. More than 100 million people
would hear him preach in his lifetime.

1816

Birth of Edward Hopper, American Presbyterian
clergyman. Pastor of several churches in New York,
Hopper is better remembered for authoring the hymn
"Jesus, Savior, Pilot Me."

1678

John Bunyan's *The Pilgrim's Progress* is published in England. Frequently imprisoned between 1660 and 1672 for preaching without a license, Bunyan used these times to collect the ideas he used in his masterpiece of Christian literature.

1546

Death of Martin Luther, German Augustinian priest and reformer. In 1517 Luther symbolically inaugurated the Protestant Reformation and remained its leader until his death. Luther also translated the Bible into German and penned the hymn "A Mighty Fortress."

1812

Congregational missionaries Adoniram and Ann Judson set sail from New England for Calcutta, India. For their subsequent work in Burma, they became two of the most famous American missionaries of their day.

1802

Birth of Leonard W. Bacon, American Congregational clergyman, educator, and editor. Bacon pastored First Congregational Church in New Haven, Connecticut (1825–81), and was a leader in the antislavery and temperance movements. He also authored the hymn "O God, Beneath Thy Guiding Hand."

1878

Italian cardinal Gioacchino Pecci is elected Pope (Leo XIII) after the death of Pope Pius IX. Leo XIII's papacy is best known for his teaching encyclicals and for the establishment of the Pontifical Biblical Commission (1902).

1743

Colonial missionary to the American Indians David Brainerd writes in his journal, "Selfish religion loves Christ for his benefits, but not for himself."

1864

St. Francis Xavier's Church in Baltimore, Maryland, the first Catholic parish church established for African-Americans, is dedicated.

1945

Death of Eric Liddell, Scottish Olympic champion runner and missionary to China. Liddell's college running days are portrayed in the 1981 film *Chariots of Fire*.

1906

Louisiana-born Baptist evangelist William J. Seymour arrives in Los Angeles and begins holding evangelistic meetings at the Apostolic Faith Mission, located at 312 Azusa Street. The "Azusa Street Revival" soon breaks out under Seymour's leadership and becomes one of the landmark events in the history of twentieth-century American Pentecostalism.

1985

Death of Alexander Scourby, American film actor, whose most memorable screen role was in *Giant* (1956). Best known for his resonant bass elocution, Scourby read the King James Version on early audiocassette tape recordings of the Bible.

1982

The U.S. Supreme Court rules that members of the Old Order Amish Church who operate businesses must pay Social Security and unemployment taxes, despite their religious belief that paying taxes is a sin.

1685

Birth of George Frideric Handel, German-born English composer of *Messiah* (first performed in 1742). He also composed hymn tunes such as "Christmas" ("While Shepherds Watched Their Flocks By Night"); "Antioch" ("Joy to the World! The Lord Is Come"); and "Maccabeus" ("Thine Be the Glory, Risen, Conquering Son").

1208

St. Francis of Assisi receives his
vocation in the Italian village of
Portiuncula. The following year he
founded the Franciscan Order, and he
is regarded by some Catholics as the
greatest of all Christian saints.

1902

Birth of English missionary Gladys Aylward. The
award-winning 1958 film *Inn of the Sixth Happiness*
(starring Ingrid Bergman) was based on Aylward's
life and work among the Chinese (1932–48).

1913

Pioneer missionary Eduard L. Arndt arrives in Shanghai, China, ten months after founding the Evangelical Lutheran Missions for China. Arndt later established mission schools in the Hankow territory and translated hymns and sermons into Chinese.

1738

English revivalist George Whitefield writes in a letter, "God, I find, has a people everywhere; Christ has a flock, though but a little flock, in all places."

1732

In Philadelphia Mass is celebrated for the first time at St. Joseph's Church, the only Roman Catholic church built and maintained in the American colonies before the American Revolutionary War. The service is led by the Reverend Joseph Greaton.

1857

Birth of Charles M. Sheldon, American Congregational clergyman, social reformer, and devotional writer. His religious novel *In His Steps* (1897) was a best seller and eventually sold 23 million copies. *In His Steps* introduced the question, "What Would Jesus Do?"

1847

The Reverend John L. Lenhart is commissioned as chaplain of the U.S. Navy. In 1862 Chaplain Lenhart became the first U.S. Navy chaplain to be killed in action, when the Confederate ironclad *Merrimac* sank the Union frigate *Cumberland* off Hampton Roads, Virginia.

1838

Birth of William J. Kirkpatrick, American Methodist sacred composer. He is best remembered for composing the melodies to such sacred favorites as "He Hideth My Soul," "'Tis So Sweet to Trust in Jesus," "Redeemed, How I Love to Proclaim It," and "Lord, I'm Coming Home."

1784

English churchman John Wesley charters a movement within Anglicanism that comes to be known as Methodism.

1865

Birth of Sir Wilfred T. Grenfell, English-born medical missionary to Labrador, Newfoundland. Grenfell built hospitals and schools, and outfitted the first hospital ship to serve fishermen in the North Sea.

1692

In colonial Massachusetts, the Salem witch trials begin with the conviction of West Indian slave Tituba for witchcraft.

1633

Beloved English clergyman and poet George Herbert dies of tuberculosis at age thirty-nine. He is best remembered as the author of the hymn "The God of Love My Shepherd Is."

1930

American missionary Gustav Herbert Schmidt (1891–1958) opens the Danzig Instytut Biblijny in the Free City of Danzig. It is the first Pentecostal Bible institute established in Eastern Europe.

1959

American Presbyterian missionary and apologist Francis A. Schaeffer observes in a letter, "Christianity is the greatest intellectual system the mind of man has ever touched."

1865

Congress approves U.S. Treasury
Secretary Salmon P. Chase's mandate
to the U.S. mint to prepare a device
with which to inscribe the motto
"In God We Trust" on U.S. coins.

1921

Death of Jessie Brown Pounds, Ohio-born Christian
poet and composer. In her lifetime Pounds authored fifty
librettos for cantatas and operettas, nine books, and more
than four hundred gospel song texts, including "Anywhere
with Jesus," "Beautiful Isle of Somewhere," "I Know That
My Redeemer Liveth," "The Way of the Cross Leads
Home," and "The Touch of His Hand on Mine."

1791

The Reverend John Hurt is appointed as the first chaplain in U.S. Army history. Hurt had previously served as chaplain of the Sixth Virginia Infantry during the American Revolution.

1738

Moravian missionary Peter Böhler advises John Wesley, "Preach faith until you have it; and then, because you have it, you will preach faith."

1743

In the midst of the Great Awakening, clergyman Thomas Prince, an avid collector of colonial historical records, publishes *The Christian History*, America's first religious magazine.

1820

Birth of Robert L. Dabney, Virginia-born theologian and educator. From his long association with Union Seminary in Virginia (1853–83), Dabney is regarded as the second-greatest theologian (after Charles Hodge) of the Southern Presbyterian Church.

1858

American Catholic reformer Isaac Hecker and his companions found the Missionary Society of St. Paul (Paulists), whose purpose is to convert Americans to Roman Catholicism.

1475

Birth of Michelangelo Buonarroti, Italian artist extraordinaire. Michelangelo's most famous works include the sculptures *Pietà* (1498) and *David* (1504), the architectural plans for rebuilding St. Peter's Cathedral in Rome, and the paintings on the 5,808-square-foot ceiling of the Sistine Chapel (1508–12).

1804

The nonsectarian British and Foreign Bible Society is founded in London "to promote the circulation of the Holy Scriptures, without note or comment, both at home and in foreign lands." BFBS funds and publications aided such missionary pioneers as William Carey, Robert Morrison, and Henry Martyn.

1825

Birth of Alfred Edersheim, Jewish-born Anglican Bible scholar, theologian, and writer. His most widely read title, *The Life and Times of Jesus the Messiah* (1883), is still in print.

1740

In Nottingham, Pennsylvania, colonial American Presbyterian revivalist Gilbert Tennent preaches his famous sermon, "The Danger of an Unconverted Ministry." Reaction by opponents of the Great Awakening produces the first split in the Presbyterian Church into Old Side and New Side factions. The two sides reunited in 1758.

1887

Death of Henry Ward Beecher, American Congregational clergyman, abolitionist, orator, and writer. The brother of Harriet Beecher Stowe, Beecher's dramatic flair made him a leading spokesman for tough social issues of the day.

1931

Clarence W. Jones and Reuben Larson incorporate the World Radio Missionary Fellowship in Lima, Ohio. It would become one of the widest-reaching radio ministries, broadcasting the gospel in many countries.

1843

Scottish clergyman Robert Murray McCheyne writes in a letter, "You will never find Jesus so precious as when the world is one vast howling wilderness. Then He is like a rose blooming in the midst of the desolation, a rock rising above the storm."

1880

English evangelist, writer, and missionary George Scott Railton, along with seven women, lands in New York City from London and inaugurates the first mission of the Salvation Army in the United States.

1898

Death of George Müller, English pastor, evangelist, philanthropist, and leader in the Christian Brethren movement. An advocate of believing prayer, Müller provided care for more than ten thousand orphans during his life, all without public appeals for support.

843

Ending an eighty-nine-year controversy, a Greek Orthodox synod repeals the iconoclastic decrees of the fifth Council of Constantinople (754), thus restoring the use of icons in Christian worship within the Eastern churches.

1847

Death of Jonathan Chapman, the American pioneer and horticultural evangelist better known as "Johnny Appleseed." Chapman's "nature theology" derived from his Swedenborgian beliefs, and he traveled throughout the Midwest, preaching and distributing apple seeds.

1904

Syrian-born Raphael Hawaweeny
is consecrated as Orthodox bishop
of Brooklyn, New York, by the
Russian patriarch Archbishop Tikhon.
Hawaweeny is thus the first Eastern
Orthodox bishop to be ordained
in America.

1607

Birth of German hymn writer Paul Gerhardt,
author of "O Sacred Head, Now Wounded."

1456

German printer Johann Gutenberg completes publication of the Bible on his printing press. It is the first copy of the scriptures produced with movable type.

1868

Birth of Charles E. Cowman, American missionary to Japan and founder of the Oriental Missionary Society. Cowman's wife, Lettie, authored the devotional classic *Streams in the Desert*.

1644

Roger Williams is granted a colonial patent by the English Parliament to found Rhode Island, the first American colony where the freedom to worship God was separated from the control of the state.

1871

American holiness author Hannah Whitall Smith writes in a letter, "It is a mistake to think we must feel good before we pray; we need to pray most of all when we feel poor, and empty, and weak."

1856

Haverford College is chartered in
Haverford, Pennsylvania: the first
Quaker college established in
the United States.

1587

Death of Caspar Olevianus, early German theologian
and reformer. He introduced the Calvinist Reformation
into parts of Germany and was a founder of the
German Reformed Church.

1952

This Week in Religion, America's first religious television program, debuts on the Dumont Television Network. Of the early religious offerings on TV, it is the only ecumenical program and airs on Sunday nights for more than two years.

1976

In an interview with Robert L. Turner, presidential candidate Jimmy Carter explains the term *born again*, "We believe that the first time we're born, as children, it's human life given to us; and when we accept Jesus as our Savior, it's a new life. That's what 'born again' means."

1856

Ex-slave Amanda Smith, renowned evangelist and missionary, is converted. She later dedicates her life to God's service at the Green Street Methodist Episcopal Church in New York and travels to England, Scotland, Liberia, and India.

1911

Death of Joseph Y. Peek, American Civil War veteran and Methodist lay preacher. He became fully ordained less than two months before his death. Peek still ministers to the church today through his hymn tune "Peek" ("I Would Be True").

1795

Bishop John Carroll ordains Demetrius A. Gallitzin (1770–1840) in Baltimore. Gallitzin is the first Catholic priest to receive full theological training in the United States and the first Catholic priest ordained in the United States.

1789

Birth of British hymnist Charlotte Elliott. Though an invalid during her last fifty years, Elliott penned 150 hymns, of which the best-known is "Just as I Am."

1953

Emmanuel Holiness Church is organized in Whiteville, North Carolina. Its founding members withdrew from the Fire-Baptized Holiness Church because they believed the parent denomination had become lax in its holiness standards.

1944

German Lutheran theologian and Nazi martyr Dietrich Bonhoeffer writes in a letter from prison, "We can have abundant life, even though many wishes remain unfulfilled."

1747

Due to his deteriorating health from tuberculosis, colonial American missionary David Brainerd ends his work among the Indians of New England.

1826

American Congregational pioneer missionary Gordon Hall dies of cholera. His enthusiasm for missions while attending Andover Seminary led to the formation in 1810 of the American Board of Commissioners for Foreign Missions. Hall was also the first American missionary to reach Mumbai, India.

1843

American Baptist lay preacher William Miller predicted that the second coming of Christ would occur on this date, but the day passes without incident. Miller adjusts his prediction of Christ's return to occur on the same date in 1844. (He was wrong again.)

1685

Birth of Johann Sebastian Bach, German Lutheran composer and musical genius. Nearly three-quarters of his one thousand compositions were written for use in Christian worship.

ca. 30

The Council of Nicaea (325) decided that Easter (the celebration of the resurrection of Jesus Christ) would be observed on the first Sunday following the first full moon after the spring equinox (March 21). This reckoning means that Easter, in any given year, will not occur earlier than March 22 nor later than April 25.

1758

American theologian Jonathan Edwards dies from a smallpox vaccination gone awry. Edwards pastored a church in Northampton, Massachusetts (1726–50), and served briefly as a missionary to the American Indians and as president of the College of New Jersey (now Princeton).

1729

First performance of Johann Sebastian Bach's "St. Matthew Passion," in Leipzig, Germany. Today, the oratorio is considered one of the most sublime masterpieces in Western music. From its score comes the haunting Good Friday hymn "O Sacred Head, Now Wounded."

1812

Birth of Stephen R. Riggs, American Board of Commissioners for Foreign Missions missionary to the Dakota Indians (1837–83). Riggs translated the Dakota language into writing, prepared a Dakota dictionary, and translated most of the Bible into the Dakota language.

1940

The first televised religious program, an Easter service officiated by Samuel Cavert of the Federal Council of the Churches of Christ in America, is broadcast by W2XBS, an NBC affiliate station in New York City.

1818

In a speech given in the House of Representatives, American statesman Henry Clay declares, "All religions united with government are more or less inimical to liberty. All separated from government are compatible with liberty."

1634

The Roman Catholic Church gains a permanent foothold in the American colonies when 128 Catholic immigrants arrive on the Potomac River from England. They settle in the colony of Maryland, founded by Cecilius Calvert, Lord Baltimore.

1906

Birth of Dawson Trotman, American Baptist youth ministry pioneer and founder of the Navigators, a youth-centered discipling ministry.

1775

American-born evangelist, mystic, and hymn writer Henry Alline undergoes a profound spiritual conversion. He later becomes a leader of the "New Light" movement in the Presbyterian Church and evangelizes the people of Nova Scotia.

1833

Birth of Greek ecclesiastic and scholar Philotheos Bryennios. In 1873 he discovered an early manuscript of the *Didache* (a second-century manual of Christian discipline, now numbered among the writings of the apostolic fathers).

1667

English Puritan poet John Milton publishes *Paradise Lost*, an epic-length poem about humanity's creation and fall.

1842

Birth of George Matheson, Scottish Free Church clergyman. Though almost blind from the age of eighteen, Matheson excelled in school and in the pulpit. Matheson also penned two enduring hymns: "O Love That Wilt Not Let Me Go" and "Make Me a Captive, Lord."

1646

Baptists hold their first recorded meeting, in Boston.

1811

Birth of John Nepomucene Neumann, Czech-born U.S. Catholic prelate. As fourth bishop of Philadelphia, Neumann organized the first Catholic diocesan school system in America. In 1963 he became the first American male saint in the Catholic Church.

1882

In Connecticut Father Michael J. McGivney charters the Knights of Columbus, a fraternal benefit society for Roman Catholic men. Today the Knights of Columbus has 1.6 million members, and its magazine, *Columbia*, has the greatest circulation of any Catholic monthly in North America.

1788

Death of Charles Wesley, cofounder of Methodism. Charles penned more than eight thousand hymns, including "O for a Thousand Tongues to Sing," "Love Divine, All Loves Excelling," "Hark! The Herald Angels Sing," "Christ the Lord is Risen Today," "Jesus, Lover of My Soul," "And Can It Be That I Should Gain," and "A Charge to Keep I Have."

1871

The Boston University School of
Theology, the first theological school
to admit women as students, is formed
by a merger of the Boston Theological
Seminary and Boston University.
(The first Bachelor of Divinity degree
awarded to a woman was granted to
Anna Oliver in 1876.)

1986

In *The Road to Daybreak* Dutch-born Catholic
priest and educator Henri J. M. Nouwen writes,
"It is such a comfort to know that Jesus' wounds
remain visible in his risen body. Our wounds are not
taken away, but become sources of hope to others."

1820

The first group of American Protestant missionaries arrives in the Sandwich Islands (now Hawaii). The party includes Hiram Bingham, Asa Thurston, Dr. Thomas Holman, Samuel Whitney, and Samuel Ruggles.

1860

Birth of Rodney "Gipsy" Smith, itinerant English evangelist. During his crusades, he visited America several times.

1745

David Brainerd begins his missionary work among the Native Americans of New Jersey, after previous efforts in Massachusetts and Pennsylvania. His New Jersey mission was his most fruitful, but he died of tuberculosis after only two years of work there.

1854

Birth of Augustine Tolton, American Catholic leader and the first black American to be ordained as a Roman Catholic priest (1886).

1524

At the age of forty, Swiss reformer and former Catholic priest Ulrich Zwingli publicly celebrates his marriage with Anna Meyer (née Reinhard) in the Zürich Cathedral. Their union lasts seven years, until Zwingli's death in the Battle of Kappel in 1531.

1827

Birth of William Holman Hunt, English painter of religious subjects and cofounder of the pre-Raphaelite Brotherhood (1848). Hunt's most famous work, *The Light of the World* (1854), represents Christ knocking at the door of the soul.

1851

Irish-born Catholic bishop John J. Hughes becomes New York's first archbishop, serving until his death in 1864. Hughes's influence leads to the establishment of a parochial school system in modern Catholic parishes.

1883

Scottish clergyman and children's novelist George MacDonald writes in a letter, "When we cannot climb the ladder of prayer, surely God comes down to the foot of it where we lie. . . . We are his and he is of our kind—only all that is infinitely better."

1507

Martin Luther is ordained as a priest in Erfurt, Germany, one year after being consecrated as a monk in the Augustinian order.

1862

Ernest W. Shurtleff, American Congregational clergyman, poet, and hymn writer is born in Boston. Shurtleff organized the American (Congregational) Church in Frankfurt, Germany (1905–06) but is better remembered as the author of the hymn "Lead On, O King Eternal."

1953

In Washington DC President Dwight D. Eisenhower inaugurates the Presidential Prayer Breakfast (later called the National Prayer Breakfast). In 1956 Eisenhower signed an act making "In God We Trust" the national motto.

1922

Death of Pandita Sarasvati Ramabai, Indian Christian educator and reformer. During a severe famine in 1896, Ramabai established an orphanage—called Mukti Sadan ("House of Salvation")—for more than three hundred women and children. She also supervised a Marathi translation of the Bible from Sanskrit.

1735

The first Moravians from Europe—
ten members of the Unitas Fratrum,
under the leadership of Augustus
G. Spangenberg, John Toltschig, and
Anton Siefert—arrive in Savannah,
Georgia, by invitation of governor
James Oglethorpe.

1810

Birth of Edmund Hamilton Sears, American Unitarian
clergyman who penned several hymns, including the
Christmas carol "It Came upon the Midnight Clear."

1628

Jonas Michaelius, the first minister of the Dutch Reformed Church to come to America, arrives in New Amsterdam (now New York City). Michaelius is best remembered for a rather mournful letter he sent to Adrian Smoutius in Amsterdam, which provides a glimpse into early colonial life.

1968

In a letter penned during the final year of his life, Swiss Reformed theologian Karl Barth writes, "How one learns to be thankful for each day on which one can still do something."

1857

A small group of Dutch immigrants, meeting in Zeeland, Michigan, organizes the Christian Reformed Church. The denomination's *Back to God Hour* radio program is now broadcast on all the major continents.

1947

Birth of Larry Norman, Christian singer and songwriter known as "the father of Christian rock." As a part of the Jesus Movement in the late 1960s, Norman was known for raising his index finger in the signature "One Way!" gesture. Norman's haunting ballad "I Wish We'd All Been Ready" has since found its way into several church hymnals.

1816

The first African Methodist Episcopal Church convention opens in Philadelphia. Sixteen delegates from five independent churches meet to form an African-American denomination based on the principles of Methodism. The following day Richard Allen is elected as the new body's first bishop.

1945

Dietrich Bonhoeffer, German Lutheran pastor and theologian is martyred by the Nazis as the result of his involvement in a plot to assassinate Adolf Hitler.

428

Nestorius is consecrated as bishop of Constantinople. When Nestorius attacked the use of the word *theotokos* (God-bearer) to describe Mary, and suggested *christotokos* (Christ-bearer) instead, he was branded a heretic.

1827

Birth of Lewis Wallace, American Civil War soldier, lawyer, diplomat, and author of *Ben Hur: A Tale of the Christ* (1880), which sold more than three hundred thousand copies in its first decade. Wallace was the best-selling religious author of his day—though he never officially joined a church.

1836

George Müller, a leader of the
Plymouth Brethren, opens his famous
orphanage on Wilson Street in Bristol,
England. By 1875 his ministry provided
care for more than two thousand
children. As a preacher at Ebenezer
Chapel, Müeller believed that material
needs could be supplied through
prayer alone; thus he abolished pew
rents and refused a salary.

1941

American Trappist monk Thomas Merton affirms
in his *Secular Journal*, "If we are willing to accept
humiliation, tribulation can become, by God's grace,
the mild yoke of Christ, His light burden."

1882

The Evangelical Reformed Church in Northwest Germany is created by royal decree when the king of Prussia orders the 124 reformed congregations scattered throughout the area (then known as the Province of Hanover) to become incorporated as an independent territorial church.

1867

Birth of Samuel M. Zwemer, American missionary to the Arab world. In 1890 Zwemer went to Arabia under sponsorship of the Syrian Mission of the Presbyterian Church in the U.S.A. He later returned to the United States and taught at Princeton Seminary.

1742

George Frideric Handel's oratorio *Messiah* is first performed in Dublin, Ireland, as an oratorio for Lent (rather than for Advent, as it is today).

1828

Birth of Joseph B. Lightfoot, Anglican prelate, Bible critic, and bishop of Durham (1879–89). Lightfoot is best remembered for his analytical work on both the New Testament and the writings of the apostolic fathers.

1813

In Philadelphia, the Religious Society of Friends (Quakers) opens the first privately operated hospital for insane patients. The Asylum for the Relief of Persons Deprived of the Use of Their Reason used no manacles, handcuffs, iron grates, or bars. In 1888 the name of the hospital was changed to the Friends Asylum for the Insane, and later to the Friends Hospital (1914).

1940

English Bible expositor Arthur W. Pink declares in a letter, "Nothing is too great and nothing is too small to commit into the hands of the Lord."

1729

German composer Johann Sebastian Bach conducts the first and only performance during his lifetime of *The Passion according to St. Matthew*, at a Good Friday vespers service at the St. Thomas Lutheran Church of Leipzig, Germany. *The St. Matthew Passion* has been called by some "the supreme cultural achievement of all Western civilization."

1452

Birth of Leonardo da Vinci, Italian Renaissance artist, scientist, and inventor. Among his more memorable paintings are *The Last Supper* (1498) and *Mona Lisa* (1503).

1922

Belvin W. Maynard, an ordained Baptist minister known as "the flying parson," delivers the first sermon preached from an airplane by radio.

1901

Death of John Jacob Esher, Evangelical United Brethren bishop and theologian. Esher was the first bishop of his denomination to visit the missions in Asia and to travel around the world.

1492

Spain's King Ferdinand and Queen Isabella give Christopher Columbus a commission to seek a westward ocean passage to Asia. Though Columbus was also interested in wealth, he saw himself as a new and true "christopher" (Christ-bearer) who would carry Christ across the oceans to a people who had not heard the gospel.

1960

Swedish Christian and secretary general of the United Nations Dag Hammarskjöld pens in his *Markings*, "Forgiveness breaks the chain of causality because he who 'forgives' you out of love takes upon himself the consequences of what you have done. Forgiveness, therefore, always entails a sacrifice."

1521

Two days after his arrival at the Diet of Worms, Martin Luther defends his doctrines and refuses to recant his teachings. When negotiations over the next few days fail to reach a compromise, Luther is condemned by the council.

1743

Death of James Blair, Scottish-born Episcopal clergyman, educator, and founder and first president of the College of William and Mary (1693–1743).

526

Justinian I is crowned Roman emperor in Constantinople's magnificent cathedral, the Santa Sophia. Attempting to restore political and religious unity in the eastern and western empires, Justinian ruthlessly attacks paganism and heretics and creates the Code of Justinian.

1836

Birth of Adoniram Judson Gordon, American Baptist clergyman, educator, and hymn composer. His better known works include "Gordon" ("My Jesus, I Love Thee"), "Clarendon" ("In Tenderness He Sought Me"), and "I Shall See the King in His Beauty." Gordon was active in missionary work and also founded what is now Gordon Divinity School.

1952

Three years after the 1949 revolution that established the People's Republic of China, evangelical leader Watchman Nee is arrested by the Chinese government and imprisoned for "corrupt business practices." Nee spends nearly all of his last twenty years in prison.

1759

Death of George F. Handel, German-born English composer. Of his religious compositions, the most famous are his *Messiah* oratorio and several hymn tunes, including "Christmas" ("While Shepherds Watched Their Flocks By Night"), "Antioch" ("Joy to the World! The Lord Is Come"), and "Maccabeus" ("Thine Be the Glory, Risen, Conquering Son").

1632

At a conference at Dordrecht, Holland, the Dutch Mennonites adopt a Confession of Faith, which comes to be known as the Dordrecht Confession of Faith.

1142

Death of Peter Abelard, French Scholastic philosopher, theologian, and educator. Abelard also wrote the hymn "O What Their Joy and Their Glory Must Be."

1864

Bronze two-cent pieces are imprinted with the words "In God We Trust," making them the first American coins to carry the motto. The motto is designed to remind the Union that the resolution of the American Civil War is in God's hands.

1907

English mystic Evelyn Underhill explains in a letter, "The material world, although an illusion in the form in which it appears to us, is an illusion which has strict relations to reality. It is the dim shadow of the thought of God. This...veil through which...we must see the Divine received its final sanction in the Incarnation of Christ."

1619

The Synod of Dort passes a five-point summary of Calvinist doctrine, which asserts (1) the total depravity of man; (2) unconditional election; (3) limited atonement; (4) the irresistibility of grace; and (5) the final perseverance of the saints. This summary has come to be known by the acronym TULIP.

1982

Death of W. Cameron Townsend, American missionary pioneer and founder of Wycliffe Bible Translators (1935). Wycliffe has since translated the New Testament into more than 130 native languages.

1886

The Reverend Augustine Tolton becomes the first African-American priest assigned to work in the United States. He is ordained at the College of Propaganda in Rome, and later opens a mission in Quincy, Illinois, in the Springfield diocese.

1576

Birth of Vincent de Paul, Catholic clergyman and philanthropist, who devoted himself to the poor and founded the missionary order of Lazarists (1625) and the Sisters of Charity (1632). Vincent helped to ransom more than one thousand Christian slaves in northern Africa. He was canonized in 1737 by Clement XII.

ca. 30

This is the latest day in the spring on which Easter can fall. (Easter is determined by the Paschal full moon, which can occur as early as March 21.) Easter has fallen on April 25 only three times during the last three centuries: 1734, 1886, and 1943. It will not occur on April 25 again until 2038.

1792

Birth of John Keble, Anglican clergyman, poet, and leader in the Oxford Movement (1833–45), which sought to purify Anglicanism. Keble is the author of the hymn "Sun of My Soul, Thou Savior Dear."

1992

Worshipers celebrate Russian
Orthodox Easter in Moscow for the
first time in seventy-four years.

1518

German reformer Martin Luther states in his disputation
of Heidelberg, "Grace is given to heal the spiritually
sick, not to decorate spiritual heroes."

1537

The First Genevan Catechism is published, which imposes itself on the inhabitants of Geneva, Switzerland. Based on John Calvin's *Institutes*, the document was compiled either by Calvin himself or by fellow French Swiss reformer Guillaume Farel.

1775

Death of Peter Böhler, the German Moravian missionary who introduced John Wesley to personal spiritual conversion and self-surrendering Christian faith. Böhler's positive, assuring faith made a permanent mark on Wesley's theology and has characterized Methodism ever since.

1960

Leaders of the one hundredth General Assembly of the Southern Presbyterian Church passes a resolution declaring that sexual relations within marriage without intentions of procreation are not sinful.

1839

Birth of Vernon J. Charlesworth, English clergyman and hymn writer. He was headmaster of Charles Spurgeon's Stockwell Orphanage but is better remembered as author of the hymn "A Shelter in the Time of Storm."

1945

Dawson Trotman begins teaching Bible memorization to American servicemen in San Pedro, California, marking the beginning of the Navigators organization. The Navigators formally incorporated in 1943 and are headquartered today in Colorado Springs.

1834

Birth of Joseph H. Gilmore, American Baptist clergyman and educator, who taught Hebrew for forty-three years at the University of Rochester. Gilmore is best remembered as the author of the hymn "He Leadeth Me, O Blessed Thought."

418

Roman Emperor Honorius (395–423) issues an imperial decree denouncing the teachings of Pelagius, who taught that human nature is able to take the initial and fundamental steps toward salvation by its own efforts, apart from empowerment by divine grace.

1739

English revivalist George Whitefield notes in his journal, "Our extremity is God's opportunity."

1886

The United Holy Church of America is founded in Method, North Carolina, a suburb of Raleigh. This predominantly African-American holiness denomination emphasizes Spirit baptism and sanctification (both regarded as works subsequent to salvation) as essential for the Christian life.

1816

Birth of Fidelia Fisk, American missionary to the Nestorians in Persia and the first principal of the women's seminary at Oroomiah.

1559

After several years on the Continent studying and writing, John Knox returns to Scotland to help lead the Scottish Reformation. The movement takes hold the following year, when queen regent Mary of Guise dies. Afterward, Knox and others drew up the Scots Confession, which Parliament approved in 1560.

373

Death of St. Athanasius the Great, bishop of Alexandria (328–73). Known today as "the father of Orthodoxy," Athanasius was the first Christian writer to list the twenty-seven books of the New Testament that we have today.

1987

Three Lutheran bodies (the Lutheran Church, the American Lutheran Church, and the Association of Evangelical Lutheran Churches) merge to form the Evangelical Lutheran Church in America, the largest Lutheran denomination in the United States. The new denomination is officially formed on January 1, 1988.

1850

Death of John Herr, Pennsylvania-born religious leader and founder of the Reformed Mennonite Church, primarily in western New York and Ontario.

1988

Biloxi-born Catholic prelate Eugene A. Marino, SSJ, is installed as archbishop of Atlanta. He is the first African-American archbishop.

1923

Death of William Robertson Nicoll, British religious journalist and editor. The son of a Scottish Free Church minister, Nicoll edited the British journal *The Expositor* and the fifty-volume *Expositor's Bible* (1888–1905).

1901

With special permission from the pope, Father Luke J. Evers conducts the first Catholic Mass for night workers at the Church of St. Andrew in New York City. Church law previously did not permit Mass before sunrise.

1813

Birth of Sören A. Kierkegaard, Danish philosopher and theologian widely regarded as "the father of existentialism." Kierkegaard attacked organized religion, holding that an individual chooses truth on the basis of (subjective) faith.

1986

The Reverend Donald E. Pelotte is ordained as the first Native American Roman Catholic bishop in Gallup, New Mexico.

1809

Birth of William Walker, Southern American music teacher and inventor of the seven-shaped-note musical system. Walker spent much of his life collecting traditional tunes of the southern Appalachians.

1787

The New Jerusalem Church is formally established by five ex-Wesleyan preachers in London. The church's theology, known popularly as Swedenborgianism, is based on the writings of Swedish scientist and mystic Emanuel Swedenborg (1688–1772).

1907

Birth of Kathryn Kuhlman, American itinerant evangelist and spiritual healer. She discovered her gift of healing while pastoring a small church in Pennsylvania, when people in her congregation began reporting unexpected healings during her services. Kuhlman's best-known book is her 1962 autobiography, *I Believe in Miracles*.

1816

In the Dutch Reformed Church in New York City, delegates from thirty-five Bible societies meet to establish the American Bible Society, which seeks to promote a wider circulation of the scriptures, unaccompanied by notes or comments.

1655

Death of Edward Winslow, English-born Puritan separatist and *Mayflower* pilgrim. A signer of the Mayflower Compact, Winslow later became governor of Plymouth Colony (1633, 1636, 1644).

1983

Pope John Paul II announces
the reversal of the Catholic Church's
1633 condemnation of Galileo Galilei,
the seventeenth-century scientist
who first espoused the Copernican
(heliocentric, or sun-centered) theory
of our solar system.

1760

Death of Nikolaus Ludwig, Count von Zinzendorf,
German Pietist reformer and pioneer in missions,
who reorganized the Unitas Fratrum into the
Moravian (Bohemian) Brethren.

1939

A Declaration of Union reunites the Methodist Church in the United States after 109 years of division. The recombined denomination comprises more than 8 million members.

1886

Birth of Karl Barth, Swiss Reformed theologian. Asked to summarize the essence of his theology, Barth once replied, "Jesus loves me this I know, for the Bible tells me so."

1825

The first national tract society in America, the American Tract Society, is organized in New York City by the merger of fifty smaller societies. By 1975 the ATS was publishing 30 million tracts a year.

1851

Birth of James M. Gray, Bible teacher and clergyman. Gray was one of the editors of the *Scofield Bible* (1909) and also served as president of Moody Bible Institute. In 1931 he helped organize the Evangelical Teacher Training Association. Gray also penned the hymn "Nor Silver Nor Gold Hath Obtained My Redemption."

1861

"The Battle Hymn of the Republic," written by Julia Ward Howe, is first performed at a flag-raising ceremony for Union recruits at Fort Warren (near Boston), during the American Civil War.

1907

English mystic Evelyn Underhill concludes in a letter, "An entire willingness to live in the dark, in pain, anything—this is the real secret. I think no one really finds the Great Companion till their love is of that kind that they long only to give and not to get."

1917

Three shepherd children near Fatima,
Portugal, report that the Virgin
Mary appeared to them. Our Lady of
Fatima—the popular title given to the
visions—is said to regularly appear to
the three children on the thirteenth of
each month between May and October.

1963

Death of A. W. Tozer, American Christian and
Missionary Alliance clergyman and Christian writer.
He served as pastor of Chicago's Southside Alliance
Church for thirty-one years. Tozer's best-remembered
writing is *The Pursuit of God* (1948).

1607

In Virginia priest Robert Hunt
presides over the first Anglican
worship service held in the New
World, on the first Sunday after the
arrival of the 120 settlers comprising
the Jamestown expedition.

1752

Birth of Timothy Dwight, American colonial clergyman
and educator. The grandson of Jonathan Edwards,
Dwight served as a chaplain in the Revolutionary War,
a Congregational clergyman in Connecticut, and later
was elected president of Yale College.

1889

The Epworth League of the Methodist Episcopal Church—the forerunner of youth ministry programs found in the United Methodist Church today—is organized during a two-day conference in Cleveland, Ohio.

1948

Death of Father Edward J. Flanagan, Irish-born parish priest, who founded the Boys Town orphanage near Omaha, Nebraska, in 1917.

1805

Anglican missionary Henry Martyn steps ashore in Calcutta, India, where he is met by William Carey. Carey soon influences Martyn to do translation work, and Martyn translates the Bible into three languages, including Hindustani, before his premature death in 1812.

1540

German reformer Martin Luther remarks, "In the worst temptations nothing can help us but faith that God's Son has put on flesh, is bone, sits at the right hand of the Father, and prays for us. There is no mightier comfort."

1881

The New Testament of the English Revised Version is published in England, the first modern English translation of the scriptures published since 1611. The product of ten years of work by fifty-four biblical scholars on both sides of the Atlantic, the ERV provided the scholarly foundation for the publication of the American Standard Version of the Bible in 1901 and 1905.

1838

Birth of William H. Hare, American Episcopal prelate and "apostle of the Sioux." He served as missionary bishop of Niobrara (Nebraska and the Dakotas) for thirty-seven years.

1843

Nearly half the member congregations of
the National Church of Scotland secede
to form the Free Church of Scotland.
Renowned clergymen associated
with this reformed Presbyterian
denomination include Thomas
Chalmers, Horatius and Andrew Bonar,
and William Robertson Smith.

1920

Birth of Karol Jozef Wojtyla, Polish Catholic cardinal,
who in 1978 was elected the first non-Italian pope
since the Renaissance, taking the name John Paul II.

1971

Godspell, a musical based on the Gospel of Matthew, opens at the Cherry Lane Theater in New York City.

1775

Anglican clergyman and hymn writer John Newton notes in a letter, "I hope you will find the Lord present at all times, and in all places. When it is so, we are at home everywhere; when it is otherwise, home is a prison, and abroad a wilderness."

325

On the site of modern Ankara, Turkey, the Council of Nicaea convenes the first ecumenical council of the Church, attended by nearly three hundred bishops. The council is called by Emperor Constantine, who seeks to establish peace and unity in the Christian Church.

1690

Death of John Eliot, English-born clergyman, Congregational missionary to colonial America, and "apostle to the American Indians," who worked with the Pequot people in Massachusetts for thirty years. Eliot's Indian language catechism (1653) was the first book printed in English in America, and his translation of the Bible into Pequot (1661–63) was the first Bible published in America.

1738

Charles Wesley is converted from a legalistic to an evangelical Christian faith. Charles entered the ministry the following year and became a gifted and tireless hymn writer known as "the sweet singer of Methodism."

1813

Birth of Robert Murray McCheyne, Scottish Presbyterian clergyman, whose pastoral letters carried spiritual influence even after McCheyne's premature death at age twenty-nine.

1541

In Germany the twenty-six-day Ratisbon Conference—seeking to unite the ideas of three Catholic theologians and three Protestant theologians— ends with tentative doctrinal agreements reached. Subsequent opposition from Martin Luther prevented any lasting reunion. After the failure of the Ratisbon Conference, the Protestant movement became permanent.

1868

Birth of William R. Newell, American Plymouth Brethren pastor and Bible teacher associated with Moody Bible Institute in Chicago. Newell is remembered today as the author of the hymn "Years I Spent in Vanity and Pride."

1955

The General Assembly of the Presbyterian Church in the United States announces that it will permit the ordination of female clergy.

1974

Russian Orthodox liturgical scholar Alexander Schmemann reflects in his journal, "The most important question is how does objective faith become subjective? How does it grow in the heart to become a personal faith? When do common words become one's own? The faith of the Church, the faith of the Fathers comes alive only when it is my own."

1950

During its annual meeting in Boston, the Northern Baptist Convention formally changes its name to the American Baptist Convention. In 1972 the denomination renamed itself the American Baptist Churches in the U.S.A.

1930

Linguistic pioneer Frank C. Laubach, serving as a Congregational missionary to the Philippines, comments in a letter, "As one makes new discoveries about his friends by being with them, so one discovers the 'individuality' of God if one entertains him continuously."

1876

The Reformed Presbyterian Church of Scotland unites with the Free Church of Scotland to form the new Free Church of Scotland.

1868

Death of "Billy" Bray of Cornwall, Welsh Methodist preacher, who for forty-three years had preached, built chapels, and taken orphans into his home.

1808

In Baltimore the Fifth American General Conference of the Methodist Episcopal Church closes. During the three-week gathering, William McKendree was ordained as the first American bishop of the Methodist Church.

735

Death of Anglo-Saxon theologian the Venerable Bede, a monk at a monastery in Jarrow, Northumberland, also known as "the father of English history." Bede was the first great English scholar. He invented the BC/AD dating system, and his *Ecclesiastical History of the English People* (731) was crucial to England's conversion to Christianity.

1917

Pope Benedict XV proclaims the *Codex Iuris Canonici* (Code of Canon Law) by papal bull. This comparatively small volume of canon law is divided into five books and 2,414 canons. It is the first redaction of the canon law to be made in the Roman Catholic Church in modern times.

1564

Death of John Calvin (born Jean Chauvin), French-born theologian and Swiss ecclesiastical reformer. Called "the organizer of Protestantism," Calvin built on the premise that the Bible is the only trustworthy source of knowledge, and thereby unified the scattered reform theologies of Europe.

1954

President Dwight Eisenhower signs into law the Congressional Act, Joint Resolution 243, which adds the words *under God* to the Pledge of Allegiance. In a speech given soon after, Eisenhower declares, in support of the new bill, "In this way we are reaffirming the transcendence of religious faith in America's heritage and future."

1640

Scottish clergyman Samuel Rutherford writes to a grieving parent, "Now the number of crosses lying in your way to glory are fewer by one than when I saw you; they must decrease."

1819

While visiting his father-in-law's church, Anglican bishop Reginald Heber pens the poetic stanzas to the hymn "From Greenland's Icy Mountains."

1874

Birth of Gilbert Keith "G. K." Chesterton, English journalist, novelist, poet, and apologist. Called "the prince of paradox" for the religious dogma underlying his light literary style, Chesterton was credited by poet T. S. Eliot with doing "more than any man in his time...to maintain the existence of the [Christian] minority in the modern world."

1971

The Provincial Council of the Russian Orthodox Church, meeting in Zagorsk, elects Metropolitan Pimen as patriarch of Moscow and all Russia.

1871

American Quaker holiness writer Hannah Whitall Smith remarks in a letter, "We Quakers are so thrifty that we do not like to live 'from hand to mouth' as the expression is. We like a stock of goodness laid up ahead, and a stock of wisdom and of patience and of all the other graces. But...God's plan for us is different. God has laid it all up for us in Christ, and we have to draw it each moment as we need it."

1821

The Cathedral of the Assumption of the Blessed Virgin Mary—the first Catholic cathedral in the United States—is dedicated in Baltimore by Archbishop Ambrose Marechal.

1699

Birth of Alexander Cruden, Scottish bookseller and compiler of *Cruden's Concordance*, first published in 1737 and still a standard reference today for the King James Version of the Bible.

1841

Scottish missionary David Livingstone departs for Africa to become a missionary explorer. Livingstone ultimately penetrated the deepest reaches of the continent, where he proclaimed the Good News.

1793

Birth of Henry Francis Lyte, Scottish Anglican clergyman, who wrote more than eighty hymns, including "Abide with Me" and "Jesus, I My Cross Have Taken."

597

Augustine, missionary to England
and first archbishop of Canterbury,
baptizes Ethelbert, the Saxon king.
Afterward the Christian faith spreads
rapidly among the Angles and Saxons.

1946

English Catholic psychiatrist Caryll Houselander
concludes in a letter, "Time is never really lost; it
is merely that sometimes it is used as God plans
instead of as we do, and we consider it to be lost!"

1162

English Catholic churchman Thomas à Becket is consecrated as archbishop of Canterbury. Becket served for eight years, until increasing ideological conflicts with King Henry II ended with Becket's martyrdom in December 1170.

1726

Birth of Philip William Otterbein, German Reformed pastor, who helped establish the Church of the United Brethren in Christ (an early branch of the modern United Methodist Church).

1948

In Manila the first missionary radio
station (FEBC) built in the Philippines
by the Far East Broadcasting Company
goes on the air. Today FEBC broadcasts
to every country in Asia, in more
than 150 languages.

1965

Death of Norwegian Old Testament scholar
Sigmund O. P. Mowinckel, who is best known for
his work on the Psalms. He also translated much
of the Old Testament into Norwegian.

988

Kiev's Grand Prince Vladimir formally
embraces the gospel, ordering
his people to be baptized into the
Orthodox Christian faith. Considered
"the apostle to the Russians," Vladimir
became the first Christian ruler of that
nation and afterward erected numerous
churches, promoted education, and
aided the poor.

1900

Birth of William E. Sangster, English Methodist preacher,
who published numerous devotional books, including
He Is Able (1936), *The Pure in Heart* (1954), and
The Secret of Radiant Life (1957).

1844

In London young merchant George Williams and twelve coworkers establish the Young Men's Christian Association. Organized to combat unhealthy conditions arising from the Industrial Revolution, the original mission of the YMCA was to improve "the spiritual condition of young men engaged in drapery and other trades."

1915

Death of William H. Cummings, English chorister and composer, who arranged the hymn tune "Mendelssohn" ("Hark! The Herald Angels Sing").

1913

Ohio-born Methodist evangelist George Bennard introduces his new hymn, "The Old Rugged Cross," during a revival meeting in Pokagon, Michigan.

1959

English apologist C. S. Lewis writes in a letter, "If we really think that home is elsewhere and that this life is a 'wandering to find home,' why should we not look forward to the arrival?"

1536

Ten Articles of Religion are published by the English clergy in support of Henry VIII's Declaration of Supremacy. The Anglican Church thus begins outlining its doctrinal distinctives, following its break with Rome.

632

Death of the Muslim prophet Mohammed, who founded Islam in 622 and wrote the Koran. Though not considered a central figure in Judeo-Christian history, Mohammed's last words are worth noting: "O God, pardon my sins. Yes, I come."

1772

Moravian missionaries build the first Protestant church west of the Alleghenies, at Schoenbrunn, in the Ohio Territory. The Reverend David Zeisberger serves as the church's first preacher.

1894

Birth of Wilbur M. Smith, American Fundamentalist Presbyterian educator. Ordained in 1922, Smith held no academic degrees, but he taught English Bible at Moody Bible Institute (1938–47), Fuller Theological Seminary (1947–63), and Trinity Evangelical Divinity School (1963–71).

1925

Canada's largest Protestant denomination, the United Church of Canada, is officially formed from the union of the Methodist Church, Canada; the Congregational Union of Canada; the Council of Local Union Churches; and about two-thirds of the Presbyterian Church of Canada. The new denomination's government is presbyterian in form.

1692

Bridget Bishop becomes the first person hanged for witchcraft during the Salem witch trials. In all, twenty people died as a result of these trials.

1799

Richard Allen is ordained as a deacon of the Methodist Episcopal Church in Philadelphia. In 1816 Allen became the founding bishop of the African Methodist Episcopal Church, making him the first African-American Protestant bishop in the United States.

1739

John Wesley, the founder of Methodism, records in his journal, "I look upon all the world as my parish."

1914

The first edition of A. T. Robertson's monumental *Grammar of the Greek New Testament* is published. Its more than fourteen hundred pages make it the largest systematic analysis of New Testament Greek ever produced.

1804

Birth of David Abeel, American missionary to the Far East. In 1829 he sailed for China under the auspices of the Seaman's Friend Society and later ministered in Java, Singapore, Siam, Malacca, Borneo, and other parts of Asia.

1793

English missions pioneer William Carey sets sail for India. Within five years, he translates nearly the entire Bible into Bengali. Today Carey is acclaimed as "the father of modern missions."

1972

American Presbyterian apologist Francis Schaeffer exhorts in a letter, "As Christians we are called upon to exhibit the character of God, and this means the simultaneous exhibition of His holiness and His love."

1966

Pope Paul VI abolishes the Vatican's *Index of Prohibited Books*, first issued by the Inquisition under Pope Paul IV in 1557. The *Index Librorum Prohibitorum* comprised a list of books that members of the Catholic Church were forbidden to read or possess.

1837

Birth of William C. Dix, English businessman and composer of several notable hymns, including "What Child Is This?" and "As with Gladness Men of Old."

1668

Padre Diego Luis de Sanvitores, a Jesuit
missionary from Mexico, establishes
the first Roman Catholic mission
on the island of Guam.

1807

Birth of William Nast, German religious leader and
founder of German Methodism. After arriving in America
in 1828, Nast organized German settlers in the Midwest
into Methodist congregations and later helped establish
German Wallace College in Berea, Ohio (which eventually
merged to become Baldwin-Wallace University).

1833

Anglican churchman John Henry
Newman pens the words to the
hymn "Lead, Kindly Light, Amid the
Encircling Gloom," while traveling by
ship from Italy to France.

1948

Death of Rufus M. Jones, American Quaker scholar,
educator, philosopher, humanitarian, and mystic,
who taught philosophy at Haverford College in
Pennsylvania (1904–34) and was a founder of the
American Friends Service Committee (1917).

1968

At a meeting in Winona Lake, Indiana, the Pilgrim Holiness Church (organized in 1897) votes to approve a merger with the Wesleyan Methodist Church of America (organized in 1843).

1859

Birth of U.S. Presbyterian evangelist J. Wilbur Chapman, first director of the Winona Lake Bible Conference Center in Indiana. Chapman also wrote the hymns "One Day When Heaven Was Filled with His Praises" and "Jesus, What a Friend of Sinners!"

1464

Pope Pius II leads a brief crusade into
Italy against the Turks. He becomes ill,
however, and dies before the rest
of his allies arrive.

1830

Birth of Elizabeth C. Clephane, an orphan who
grew up in the Free Church of Scotland and became a
humanitarian and a poet. Clephane authored two of the
more haunting hymns in the church today: "Beneath the
Cross of Jesus" and "The Ninety and Nine."

325

The Council of Nicaea closes. By the end of the month-long assembly—the church's first ecumenical council, called by Pope Sylvester I and Roman emperor Constantine I—the three hundred assembled bishops had formulated the Nicene Creed, condemned the Arian heresy (which denied the deity of Christ), and established the method for calculating the date of Easter.

1834

Birth of Charles Haddon Spurgeon, English Baptist preacher and one of the greatest public speakers of his day. His London congregation grew to six thousand members, and his published sermons fill more than fifty large volumes.

1885

A band of Moravian missionaries lands on the shores of Alaska and establishes the Bethel Mission. During their first year of mission work among the natives, winter temperatures fell to fifty degrees below zero.

1779

Birth of Dorothy Ann Thrupp, English devotional writer. She is best remembered as the author of the hymn "Savior, Like a Shepherd Lead Us."

1821

The African Methodist Episcopal Zion Church is formally constituted in New York City, with nineteen clergymen present, representing six African-American churches from New York, Philadelphia, New Haven, and Newark.

1821

Birth of Henry W. Baker, English clergyman, musicologist, and compiler of *Hymns Ancient and Modern*—regarded today as the unofficial Anglican church hymnal. Baker also authored a hymn based on Psalm 23: "The King of Love My Shepherd Is."

1750

New England Congregational
clergyman Jonathan Edwards
is dismissed from his pulpit in
Northampton, Massachusetts, after
twenty-three years. Edwards's
ultraconservative theology had become
too theologically and administratively
inflexible for his congregation.

1745

David Brainerd, colonial-era missionary to New
England Native Americans, writes in his journal, "I am
often weary of this world, and want to leave it on
that account; but it is more desirable to be drawn,
rather than driven out of it."

1683

English Quaker colonizer William Penn signs his famous treaty with the Native Americans of Pennsylvania.

1738

Birth of Samuel Medley, English Baptist clergyman and author of the hymns "O Could I Speak the Matchless Worth" and "I Know That My Redeemer Lives."

1941

The two-day Constitutional Assembly of the Nippon Kirisuto Kyodan opens, during which the United Church of Christ in Japan is formed. Today one-third of all Japanese Protestants belong to the United Church.

1542

Birth of St. John of the Cross, Spanish Carmelite monk, mystic, and poet. A founder of the Discalced Carmelites, he authored the religious classic *The Dark Night of the Soul*. He was canonized by Pope Benedict XIII in 1726.

1530

The principal creed of Lutheranism, the Augsburg Confession, is first presented to Emperor Charles V at the Diet of Augsburg. Prepared chiefly by Philipp Melanchthon, its *Twenty-one Articles* later influenced the Anglicans' *Thirty-Nine Articles* and John Wesley's *Twenty-three (Methodist) Articles*.

1842

Birth of Daniel S. Warner, American churchman and founder of the Church of God (Anderson, Indiana).

1968

The Wesleyan Church (a noncharismatic American holiness denomination) is formed by the union of the Wesleyan Methodist Church (organized in 1843) and the Pilgrim Holiness Church (which began as the International Holiness Union and Prayer League in 1897).

1839

Scottish clergyman and missionary Robert Murray McCheyne writes in a letter, "Joy is increased by spreading it to others."

1736

As a member of the Holy Club
(to which John and Charles Wesley
also belonged), future English
revivalist George Whitefield preaches
his first sermon, at the age of twenty-
one. Whitefield went on to preach
thousands more sermons and became
a force in colonial America's
"Great Awakening."

1818

Birth of James L. Breck, American Episcopal missionary
to the Wisconsin Territory. In 1859 one of Breck's
converts, Enmegahbowh, became the first Ojibwa Indian
to be ordained in the Episcopal Church. Breck was also a
founder of Seabury Seminary, near St. Paul, Minnesota.

1629

The Peace of Alais is signed, ending the Huguenot Wars in France. By this treaty, French Protestants obtained religious freedom of conscience but lost military advantage in their French homeland.

1851

Birth of Eliza E. Hewitt, American Presbyterian church worker and devotional author. Four of her hymns are still sung: "Will There Be Any Stars?" "More about Jesus Would I Know," "When We All Get to Heaven," and "Sunshine in the Soul."

1875

The first holiness conference opens at Keswick, England, emphasizing a noncharismatic "crisis" form of sanctification, in contrast to the older, Calvinist view of sanctification as a lifelong process.

1757

Anglican clergyman and hymn writer John Newton offers this encouragement in a letter: "Whatever we may undertake with a sincere desire to promote His glory, we may comfortably pursue. Nothing is trivial that is done for Him."

1629

The settlers of Salem, Massachusetts, appoint Samuel Skelton as their pastor. Their church covenant, composed by Skelton, establishes Salem as the first nonseparating Congregational Puritan Church in New England.

1315

Martyrdom of Raymond Lull, a Spanish mystic, who devoted his life as a missionary to the Islamic people. Lull first traveled to North Africa in 1291.

1899

In Boscobel, Wisconsin, the Christian Commercial Men's Association of America is formed by three traveling businessmen: John H. Nicholson, Samuel E. Hill, and William J. Knights. Known today as the Gideons, the organization placed its first Bible at the Superior Hotel in Iron Mountain, Montana, in 1908.

1811

Birth of William J. Boone, the first American Protestant Episcopal missionary bishop to China. He arrived in 1837 and settled in Shanghai in 1845, where he remained until his death. Two of Boone's sons also became missionaries.

1973

Lieutenant Florence Dianna Pohlman of La Jolla, California, is sworn in at Newport, Rhode Island, as the first female Navy chaplain. She was later assigned to the Naval Training Center in Orlando, Florida.

1489

Birth of Thomas Cranmer, first Protestant archbishop of Canterbury. Cranmer nullified several of King Henry VIII's marriages, maintained the divine right of kings, and promoted translation of the Bible into the common vernacular. He was also the primary author of the 1549 *Book of Common Prayer*. When Queen Mary ascended to the throne of England, Cranmer was condemned for treason and burned at the stake.

1878

Lutheran Church—Missouri Synod missionaries J. Friedrich Doescher and Fredrick Berg establish the Negro Lutheran Church in Little Rock, Arkansas, the first formal outreach to African-Americans made by Lutherans in the United States.

1756

English Methodism founder John Wesley writes in a letter, "One who lives and dies in error, or in dissent from our Church, may yet be saved; but one who lives and dies in sin must perish."

993

Ulrich of Augsburg, the first official Roman Catholic saint, is canonized. Prior to this, saints were declared by popular consensus.

1870

Birth of Scottish theologian James Moffatt, who pastored in Scotland's Free Church (1894–1907) and later taught at Union Seminary in New York City (1927–39). Moffatt is most widely remembered for publishing a translation of the Bible in modern, colloquial English in the 1920s.

1865

In London pioneer English revivalist William Booth holds the first "rescue meeting" at his newly established Christian Mission. In 1878 Booth changed the name of his organization to the Salvation Army.

1962

Death of H. Richard Niebuhr, American Neo-orthodox theologian. Regarded as more scholarly than his older brother, Reinhold, Richard taught Christian ethics at Yale University for thirty years. His best-known work is *Christ and Culture* (1951).

1054

The medieval church suffers a permanent fracture when the four eastern patriarchates—Constantinople, Alexandria, Jerusalem, and Antioch— break fellowship with the western patriarchate in Rome, marking the beginning of the Great Schism between the Roman Catholic and Eastern Orthodox churches.

1905

Birth of Harold J. Ockenga, American Congregational minister and evangelical leader. He served as the first president of the National Association of Evangelicals and was cofounder of Fuller Theological Seminary in California.

1946

Frances Xavier Cabrini (1850–1917) is canonized by Pope Pius XII as the first American citizen to be made a saint in the Roman Catholic Church. Known as Mother Cabrini, she founded the Institute of the Missionary Sisters of the Sacred Heart and helped establish hospitals, schools, and orphanages throughout the United States and in South America.

1787

Birth of César H. A. Malan, French-born Swiss clergyman, who penned more than one thousand hymns, including the words to "Take My Life and Let It Be" and the hymn tune "Hendon" ("Ask Ye What Great Thing I Know").

1835

The American Liberty Bell cracks
while tolling the death of Chief
Justice John Marshall. The bell had
been cast in England in 1752 and bore
an inscription from Leviticus 25:10:
"Proclaim liberty throughout all the
land unto all the inhabitants thereof."

1115

Death of French preacher Peter the Hermit, whose
report to Pope Urban II of atrocities that Seljuk Turks
were inflicting on Christian pilgrims to the Holy Land
led to Urban's fiery pronouncement of the First
Crusade at the Council of Clermont in 1095.

1962

Two hundred fifty Protestant and Orthodox delegates from eighty-one countries attend the third World Institute on Christian Education in Belfast, Northern Ireland.

381

Birth of Nestorius, first patriarch of Constantinople, who was deposed for heresy by the Council of Ephesus in 431 for teaching that Jesus Christ had two natures and two persons (rather than two natures in one person).

1925

The Scopes Monkey Trial opens in Dayton, Tennessee, with Clarence Darrow defending John Scopes from charges of teaching evolution in his high school biology classroom, contrary to Tennessee law. At trial's end, Scopes was found guilty and fined one hundred dollars.

1746

David Brainerd, colonial-era missionary to the American Indians, reflects in his journal, "I saw plainly there was nothing in the world worthy of my affection— my heart was dead to all below; yet not through dejection. . .but from a view of a better inheritance."

1656

Ann Austin and Mary Fisher, the first Quakers to arrive in America, land at Boston. They are promptly arrested by Massachusetts authorities and deported back to England five weeks later.

1955

American Presbyterian missionary and apologist Francis Schaeffer concludes in a letter, "No price is too high to pay to have a free conscience before God."

1739

David Brainerd undergoes a personal conversion experience. He was later commissioned by the Society for the Propagation of Christian Knowledge as a missionary to the New England Indians.

1536

Death of Dutch humanist and scholar Desiderius Erasmus, leader of the Renaissance in northern Europe. Erasmus opposed the fanaticism of the Reformation, choosing to reform the church from within, through scholarship and Christian instruction. His critical satire *In Praise of Folly* (1509) demonstrated the need for reform. His *Greek New Testament* (1516) encouraged the church to go beyond its Latin (Vulgate) roots.

1727

Count Nikolaus Zinzendorf organizes the Bohemian Protestant refugees on his land into the Moravian community of Unitas Fratrum (United Brethren).

1886

Birth of Edward Flanagan, Irish-born Roman Catholic parish priest who founded the Home for Homeless Boys outside Omaha, Nebraska, which was later renamed Boys Town.

1892

The Baptist Young People's Union
holds its first annual national
convention in Detroit, Michigan.

1768

Birth of Scottish evangelist James A. Haldane,
who founded the Society for the Propagation
of the Gospel at Home in 1797.

1549

Led by Francis Xavier, Spanish Jesuits land in Kagoshima, becoming the first Christian missionaries to Japan. The next ninety years came to be known as "the Christian century of Japan."

1802

Death of Scottish-born colonial printer Robert Aitken, whose presses produced the first American edition of the King James Version of the New Testament, making it the first English Bible printed in America.

1937

In eastern Germany, near Weimar, the Nazis open a concentration camp at Buchenwald. Over the next eight years (before the camp was liberated by U.S. soldiers in April 1945), nearly fifty-seven thousand prisoners would die at Buchenwald.

1944

German Lutheran theologian and Nazi martyr Dietrich Bonhoeffer observes in a letter from prison, "One has to live for some time in a community to understand how Christ is 'formed' in it (Galatians 4:19)."

1505

In Germany twenty-one-year-old Martin Luther enters the Erfurt monastery of the Augustinian Eremites. Having survived a lightning strike, Luther vowed to become a monk, took his vows in 1506, and was ordained a priest in 1507.

1674

Birth of Isaac Watts, English Nonconformist clergyman and pioneer hymn writer. Regarded as the father of English hymnody, Watts penned more than 750 songs, including "When I Survey the Wondrous Cross," "Come, We that Love the Lord," "We're Marching to Zion," "I Sing the Almighty Power of God," "Alas! and Did My Savior Bleed," "My Shepherd Will Supply My Need," and "Joy to the World!"

64

Roman emperor Nero blames Christians for an extensive fire that destroys most of the city of Rome. His accusation brings about the first great wave of persecution on the Church.

1681

Death of Georg Neumark, German educator, hymnist, and composer. Twice during his life he lost everything he owned—once to robbers and once to fire. Neumark wrote the hymn "If Thou but Suffer God to Guide Thee."

1913

The first Victorious Life Conference convenes in Oxford, Pennsylvania. Inspired by the Keswick Conferences held in England (beginning in 1875) and the Northfield Conferences in the United States (beginning in 1880), the Victorious Life Conference promotes the belief that a Christian can gain immediate freedom from the power of every known sin.

1961

U.N. secretary general Dag Hammarskjöld of Sweden prays in his journal, *Markings*, "Give us a pure heart, That we may see Thee, A humble heart, That we may hear Thee, A heart of Love, That we may serve Thee, A heart of faith, That we may live Thee, Thou, Whom I do not know, but Whose I am."

1726

Colonial American Puritan clergyman Jonathan Edwards, age twenty-three, marries fellow Puritan Sarah Pierpont, age sixteen. Their marriage prospered through the next thirty-two years in a joint, active ministry, before Jonathan's premature death in 1758.

1922

Death of Belle Harris Bennett, missions leader and social reformer of the American Southern Methodist Church. In 1892 she helped to found Scarritt College for Christian Workers (which closed in 1988). The campus in Nashville is now the Scarritt-Bennett Center.

1900

Albert Schweitzer receives his
licentiate in theology. He later
became famous as a musicologist,
physician, and missionary.

1829

Birth of Priscilla Jane Owens, American public school
teacher and hymn writer. She lived her entire life in
Baltimore, where she taught for forty-nine years.
She also published a number of articles and poems
during her lifetime, including the hymn texts
"We Have an Anchor" and "Jesus Saves."

1620

Pastor John Robinson and a band of separatist Puritans from England, who had taken refuge in the Netherlands, leave Holland for England to emigrate to America. This congregation afterward became known as the Pilgrims.

1849

Birth of Emma Lazarus, American Jewish poet and essayist. In 1883 she authored the poem "The New Colossus," which is inscribed on the base of the Statue of Liberty.

1825

Kidnapped earlier by Muslim slave traders from his Yoruba homeland in north-central Africa, Samuel Adjai Crowther is rescued by English missionaries and baptized into the Church. In 1864 Crowther was consecrated as missionary bishop of the Niger Territory.

1834

Birth of American Catholic prelate James Gibbons, archbishop of Baltimore from 1877–1921. He was also the founder and first chancellor of the Catholic University of America in Washington DC.

1216

Cardinal Cencio Savelli is consecrated as Pope Honorius III. During his pontificate, he confirmed two well-known religious orders: the Dominicans (1216) and the Franciscans (1223).

1725

Birth of John Newton, Anglican clergyman and hymn writer. Master of a slave ship for ten years, before his conversion to Christianity in 1747, Newton later studied for Anglican ordination and was appointed curate at Olney in 1764. There he became a friend of poet William Cowper, and together they published *Olney Hymns* (1779), which included such well-known hymns by Newton as "Amazing Grace" and "Glorious Things of Thee Are Spoken."

1968

Pope Paul VI publishes *Humanae Vitae*, an encyclical condemning all forms of birth control except the "rhythm method."

1848

Birth of Arthur J. Balfour, British statesman and philosopher, who served as British prime minister from 1902 to 1905, and later as foreign secretary. In 1917 he issued the Balfour Declaration, which favored the creation of "a national home for the Jewish people" in Palestine.

1603

James VI of Scotland becomes James I of England. He had been Scotland's king since 1567, but when Elizabeth I of England died, James's descent from Henry VIII made him the nearest heir to the English throne. Among his numerous acts affecting religious life in England was the royal order that led to publication of the Authorized (King James) Bible in 1611.

1933

Death of Charles A. Tindley, African-American clergyman and hymn writer. Born of slave parents and orphaned at age five, Tindley taught himself to read and write. He later studied theology and in 1885 was ordained to the Methodist ministry. As a writer of gospel songs, his most moving hymns include "By and By," "Leave It There," "Nothing Between," and "Stand by Me."

1516

Future reformer Martin Luther preaches for the first time against indulgences. It was Luther's posting of his "Ninety-five Theses" against indulgences and other church abuses that ultimately precipitated the Protestant Reformation.

1741

Birth of Francois H. Barthélémon, violinist and hymn composer, who wrote five operas, six symphonies, and one oratorio, as well as numerous concertos and violin sonatas. Two of his compositions became hymn tunes: "Autumn" ("Hail, Thou Once Despised Jesus") and "Balerma" ("Oh, for a Closer Walk with God").

1648

The General Assembly of the Church of Scotland adopts the Westminster Shorter Catechism. This document, as well as the Westminster Larger Catechism, both compiled in 1647, have been in regular use among Presbyterians, Congregationalists, and Baptists ever since.

1960

American Trappist monk Thomas Merton confesses in a letter, "I can depend less and less on my own power and sense of direction—as if I ever had any. But the Lord supports and guides me without my knowing how, more and more apart from my own action and even in contradiction to it."

1974

In Philadelphia eleven women are ordained as Episcopal priests in the Church of the Advocate. The ordination was later ruled invalid by the House of Bishops, but on October 17, 1974, the House approved in principle the ordination of women as priests. The ordinations of the eleven women were finally approved on September 16, 1976.

1912

Birth of Clarence Jordan, founder of Koinonia Farm in Americus, Georgia. Jordan's *Cotton Patch Gospel*, published in four volumes (1968–73), paraphrases the New Testament (except for Revelation) in the Southern vernacular and setting.

1822

African-American clergyman James Varick is consecrated as the first bishop of the African Methodist Episcopal Zion Church.

1718

Death of William Penn, English Quaker statesman and colonial leader. Penn's Frame of Government for the American colony of Pennsylvania (1682) established the structure for religious and political freedom in the colony. Penn's best-known writing is the ethically challenging *No Cross, No Crown* (1669).

1970

The complete New American Standard Version of the Bible is published. (The NASB New Testament first appeared in 1963.)

1889

Death of Horatius Bonar, Scottish Free Church clergyman, hymnist, and influential scholar. He authored numerous books but is remembered chiefly as a hymn writer. Of the more than six hundred hymns he authored, one hundred are still in use, including "Here, O My Lord, I See Thee Face to Face."

1652

Nikita Minin is elected as Nikon, patriarch of Moscow. He was later deposed by the Council of Moscow (1666) and banished. Nikon's view that spiritual power supersedes temporal might was a factor in Peter the Great's decision to abolish the patriarchy.

1953

British literary scholar and Christian apologist C. S. Lewis writes in a letter, "How little people know who think that holiness is dull. When one meets the real thing, it is irresistible."

1907

The Vatican issues the *Ne Temere* decree, declaring that Catholic marriages are valid only if celebrated before a duly qualified priest and at least two witnesses.

1788

Birth of Joseph J. Gurney, English banker, philanthropist, and leading evangelical Quaker theologian of the early nineteenth century. Gurney was a descendant of Quaker theologian Robert Barclay, and the brother of prison reformer Elizabeth Fry.

1785

The Reverend Ashbel Baldwin
becomes the first Episcopalian
ordained in the United States,
in Middleton, Connecticut.

1858

Birth of Maltbie D. Babcock, American
Presbyterian clergyman and hymn writer.
Babcock is remembered today as the author
of the hymn "This is My Father's World."

1874

U.S. Methodist pastor John H. Vincent and manufacturer Lewis Miller establish the Chautauqua Organization, in Fair Point, New York. Beginning as a two-week summer retreat for training Sunday school teachers, the Chautauqua Assembly grew to include additional lectures and entertainment addressing all branches of popular education.

1792

Birth of Edward Irving, Scottish theologian, mystic, and religious leader. Irving acquired fame as a preacher, but in 1832 he was condemned as a heretic and compelled to resign from his church because of his acceptance of Pentecostal phenomena.

1604

Baptism of John Eliot, English-born
Congregational missionary who
came to Massachusetts in 1631 and
became the "apostle to the Indians."
Eliot translated the scriptures
into the Pequot language, and also
helped establish the Society for the
Propagation of the Gospel in
New England.

1900

Death of James A. Healy, the first
African-American Catholic bishop.

1774

English religious leader Ann Lee and a small band of followers arrive in America at New York City. Her sect, the United Society of Believers in Christ's Second Appearing, is commonly known as the Shakers.

1966

Swiss Reformed theologian Karl Barth affirms in a letter, "Since God does in fact address man in His Word, He obviously regards him as addressable in spite of the fact that man as a sinner closes his ears and heart to Him."

1560

Ratification of the Scots Confession
by the Scottish Parliament marks the
triumph of the Reformation in Scotland,
under the leadership of John Knox.

1894

Death of James Strong, American Methodist biblical
scholar and editor. His chief contribution to scholarship
was as editor of the twelve-volume *Cyclopaedia of Biblical,
Theological, and Ecclesiastical Literature* (1867–87). He
is also remembered as compiler of *Strong's Exhaustive
Concordance of the Bible*.

1852

The roots of the Baptist General Conference are planted in Rock Island, Illinois, when Swedish immigrant pastor Gustaf Palmquist baptizes his first three converts in the Mississippi River.

1539

German reformer Martin Luther remarks in a sermon, "Reason does not know that salvation must come down from above; we want to work up from below so that the satisfaction is rendered by us."

1973

In Asheville, North Carolina, delegates
from two hundred congregations
vote to sever ties with the Southern
Presbyterian Church (PCUS),
believing it has become too liberal.
A new denomination—the National
Presbyterian Church—was formed,
and became the Presbyterian Church
in America in 1974.

1788

Birth of Adoniram Judson, pioneer American Baptist
missionary to Burma. Judson translated the Bible
into Burmese and also penned the hymn
"Come, Holy Spirit, Dove Divine."

1933

Wycliffe Bible Translators gets its start at the Day of Prayer for the Tribes of Latin America in Keswick, New Jersey. Founders W. Cameron Townsend and Leonard L. Legters incorporated WBT in 1942, and it has since grown into one of the largest interdenominational missionary agencies in the world.

1960

Death of Ralph S. Cushman, American Methodist bishop, author, and poet. His best-known verse begins, "I met God in the morning when my day was at its best; and His Presence came like sunrise, like a glory in my breast."

1760

Irish-born English minister Philip Embury arrives in New York, making him the first Methodist clergyman to come to America. In 1768 he founded Wesley Chapel.

1933

Birth of Jerry Falwell, U.S. Baptist clergyman and founding pastor of Thomas Road Baptist Church in Lynchburg, Virginia. In 1979 Falwell founded the Moral Majority, a Christian political lobbying organization.

1950

Pope Pius XII issues the *Humani Generis* encyclical, which denounces certain modernist intellectual tendencies within Catholic theology, including existentialism, excessive emphasis on scripture to the detraction of reason, contempt for the authority of the Church, distrust of scholastic philosophy, and denial that Adam existed as a historical person.

1715

Death of Nahum Tate, British poet and dramatist, who wrote the *New Version of the Psalms of David* (1696) and authored the popular Christmas carol "While Shepherds Watched Their Flocks."

1682

The first Welsh immigrants to
the American colonies arrive in
Pennsylvania and settle near
modern-day Philadelphia.

1919

Birth of Rex Humbard, American pioneer radio
and television evangelist. In 1958 he established the
Cathedral of Tomorrow in Akron, Ohio, which
became the base for his early television ministry.

1248

Rebuilding of the Cologne Cathedral—
the largest Gothic-style cathedral in
Northern Europe—begins in Germany.
The cathedral was first built in 873 but
was destroyed by fire. The rebuilding
project was completed exactly 632
years later, on August 14, 1880. The
cathedral was damaged again
during World War II.

1810

Birth of Samuel Sebastian Wesley, English organist and
hymn composer. The grandson of Charles Wesley, Samuel
Wesley composed more than 130 original hymn tunes,
including "Aurelia" ("The Church's One Foundation").

1456

After a two-year printing process, Henry Cremer finishes binding the first volume of the two-volume *Gutenberg Bible*. At its completion, the *Gutenberg Bible* became both the first full-length book to be printed in the West, and the first printed edition of the scriptures.

1613

Birth of Jeremy Taylor, English bishop, theologian, and devotional writer. Two of Taylor's writings became classic expressions of Anglican spirituality: *The Rule and Exercise of Holy Living* (1650) and *The Rule and Exercise of Holy Dying* (1651).

1972

Philip A. Potter, a West Indian
Methodist clergyman, is named
general secretary of the World
Council of Churches.

.

1942

Birth of Don Wyrtzen, American contemporary
Christian songwriter. Among his most enduring
compositions are "Yesterday, Today, and Tomorrow,"
"Worthy Is the Lamb," and "Love Was When."

1635

English Puritan Richard Mather arrives in Boston. A staunch defender of congregational church government, Mather was the father of a ministerial "dynasty" that included his son, Increase Mather (born in 1639) and grandson Cotton Mather (born in 1663).

1761

Birth of William Carey, pioneer English missionary to India. Carey taught at Fort William College in Calcutta from 1801 until his death in 1834, and helped establish Serampore Press, which made the Bible accessible to more than 300 million people.

1927

Twenty-year-old Theodore Epp is converted to a living faith. A pioneer in Christian radio broadcasting, Epp founded *Back to the Bible*, an evangelistic radio program, in 1939. *Back to the Bible* is now heard on more than six hundred stations around the world.

1959

Death of Haldor Lillenas, American hymn writer, who founded Lillenas Music Company (1924) and authored nearly four thousand gospel texts and hymn tunes, including "Wonderful Grace of Jesus" and "Peace, Peace, Wonderful Peace."

1886

Baptist clergyman Richard G. Spurling establishes the Christian Union in Monroe County, Tennessee. In 1923 this Pentecostal denomination changed its name to Church of God (Cleveland, Tennessee).

1843

Birth of Cyrus I. Scofield, American Congregational lawyer and biblical lecturer, who taught that seven distinct dispensations of God's relationship to man are revealed in scripture. Scofield's most enduring contribution to Christian studies was his *Scofield Reference Bible* (1909).

1874

Theodore Tilton, American newspaper editor, poet, and abolitionist, files charges against renowned Congregational clergyman Henry Ward Beecher for alleged adultery with Mrs. Tilton. Beecher was exonerated by the Congregational Council in 1876, after a sensational trial ended with a hung jury.

1553

Protestant reformer John Calvin concludes in a letter, "Seeing that a Pilot steers the ship in which we sail, who will never allow us to perish even in the midst of shipwrecks, there is no reason why our minds should be overwhelmed with fear and overcome with weariness."

1912

William Bramwell Booth, son of
founder William Booth, becomes head
of the American Salvation Army.

1841

Birth of Frederick C. Atkinson, English sacred
organist and choirmaster. Atkinson composed
several Anglican anthems, instrumental pieces,
and hymn tunes, including "Morecambe"
("Spirit of God, Descend Upon My Heart").

1968

Pope Paul VI arrives in Colombia
for the first ever papal visit
to South America.

1953

English psychiatrist Caryll Houselander confides
in a letter to a friend, "What a wonderful thing
God's love is, always overflowing, always following
you and, if one may say so, spoiling you."

1948

The World Council of Churches is founded in Amsterdam, with 147 member churches. It soon establishes its headquarters in Geneva, Switzerland.

1882

Death of Charles W. Fry, original bandmaster of the English Salvation Army. Fry is remembered today as the author of the hymn "Lily of the Valley" (or "I Have Found a Friend in Jesus").

1970

Editors and scholars at the Catholic
University of America in Washington
DC publish the New American Bible,
which replaces the traditional
1610 Rheims-Douay version of
the scriptures.

1747

Birth of John A. Dickins, pioneer church leader
who first suggested the denominational name
Methodist Episcopal Church.

1817

Joseph Mohr begins serving as pastor
of St. Nicholas Church in Oberndorf,
Austria. In 1818, on Christmas Eve,
Mohr and church organist Franz
Gruber created the enduring Christmas
carol "Stille Nacht" ("Silent Night").

1864

Birth of John Henry Jowett, English
Congregational clergyman and pastor of
Westminster Chapel in London (1918–23).

1901

The New Testament of the American Standard Version Bible is published. This U.S. edition of the 1881 English Revised Version comprises the first major American Bible translation.

1832

Death of Adam Clarke, British Wesleyan preacher and theologian. Clarke helped to establish Methodism in the Shetland Islands and served on the British and Foreign Bible Society. He is best known as the author of an eight-volume commentary on the Bible (1810–26), which is still reprinted today.

1876

Thirteen-year-old G. Campbell
Morgan delivers his first sermon.
He later became one of the most
renowned expository preachers and
writers of the late nineteenth and
early twentieth centuries.

1910

Birth of Albanian nun Agnes G. Bojaxhiu, better
known as Mother Teresa of Calcutta. She joined the
Sisters of Loreto in 1928, and from 1948 spent her life
ministering to the poor of India. Mother Teresa won
the Nobel Peace Prize in 1979.

1953

Founder Bill Bright incorporates Campus Crusade for Christ, in Los Angeles. Today CCC trains evangelical Christian leaders in more than ninety countries around the world.

430

Death of Augustine of Hippo, an early Latin church father and one of the outstanding theological figures of the ages. It was Augustine who wrote, "Thou hast made us for thyself, O Lord, and our hearts are restless till they find their rest in thee."

1867

The Social Brethren, a small,
evangelistic denomination,
is officially organized in Illinois.

1792

Birth of American revivalist and educator
Charles G. Finney, who served as president
of Oberlin College from 1851 to 1866.

1856

The Methodist Episcopal Church establishes Wilberforce University, in Xenia, Ohio. Ownership of the school was transferred to the African Methodist Episcopal (AME) Church in 1863.

1859

Birth of John Taylor Hamilton, British West Indies–born American Moravian bishop, educator, and historian of the Moravian Church. Hamilton taught at Moravian College and Theological Seminary, Bethlehem, Pennsylvania (1886–1903), and later served as its president (1918–28).

1954

The second assembly of the World Council of Churches closes in Evanston, Illinois. The fifteen hundred participants included five hundred delegates from 163 Protestant and Orthodox churches. (Roman Catholics were banned from attending by Cardinal Samuel A. Stritch, archbishop of Chicago.)

1688

Death of English separatist clergyman John Bunyan, author of two English-language masterpieces: *Grace Abounding to the Chief of Sinners* (1666) and *The Pilgrim's Progress* (1678).

1836

Missionaries Marcus Whitman and Henry H. Spalding reach Fort Walla Walla on the Columbia River and establish the first U.S. settlement in the territory of northern Oregon. Their wives, Narcissa Whitman and Eliza Spalding, were the first white women to cross the American continent.

1785

Birth of pioneer circuit rider Peter Cartwright, perhaps the best known of the early Methodist preachers along the American frontier. Cartwright later served in the Illinois state legislature and was defeated in an 1846 race for Congress by Abraham Lincoln.

1921

The first general synod of the African Orthodox Church convenes in New York City. This branch of the Protestant Episcopal Church was established in 1919 by George A. McGuire, who was also elected the denomination's first bishop.

1973

Death of J. R. R. Tolkien, English philologist and fantasy novelist. A devout Catholic, Tolkien wrote *The Hobbit* (1937) and The Lord of the Rings trilogy (1954–55).

1752

This date became September 14 when Great Britain (including Scotland, Ireland, Wales, and the American colonies) officially adopted the Gregorian calendar—developed by Pope Gregory XIII in 1582 to replace the older, now inaccurate, Julian calendar.

1995

Dutch-born Catholic priest and educator Henri J. M. Nouwen confides in his journal, "Prayer connects my mind with my heart, my will with my passions, my brain with my belly.... Prayer is the divine instrument of my wholeness, unity, and inner peace."

1847

Scottish Anglican clergyman Henry Francis Lyte pens the words to his last (and best-known) hymn: "Abide with Me: Fast Falls the Eventide."

1803

Birth of Sarah Childress Polk, American Presbyterian fundamentalist and wife of U.S. president James K. Polk. Mrs. Polk banned dancing at presidential functions and was the first First Lady to institute a strict Sabbath observance.

1810

The American Board of Commissioners for Foreign Missions is formally organized by the Congregational churches of New England at Farmington, Connecticut. It is the first foreign missions society established in America.

1802

Birth of Frederick Oakeley, an Anglican clergyman who became a Catholic during the time of the Oxford Movement (1845). Oakeley authored several volumes of poetry, and his translation of the Latin "Adeste Fidelis" gave the Church the popular carol "O Come, All Ye Faithful."

1620

With 101 passengers aboard, the *Mayflower* sails from Plymouth, England, bound for the New World. The ship was ninety feet long and twenty-six feet wide. Two months and five days later, the ship landed near modern-day Cape Cod, Massachusetts.

1529

Martyrdom of George Blaurock, early Swiss Anabaptist evangelist. Blaurock helped to plant the Anabaptist faith throughout much of central Europe before he was arrested and burned for heresy.

1724

In Germantown, Pennsylvania, the first congregation of German Dunkards (so called for their practice of baptism by three-time immersion) is formed, led by Peter Becker. The group originated in Schwarzenau, Germany, in 1708. Their official name, Church of the Brethren, was adopted in 1908.

1559

Death of Robert Estienne (also known as Robertus Stephanus and Robert Stephens), French scholar and printer who in 1551 became the first to print the Bible with modern verse divisions.

1974

At the Naval Air Station in Atlanta, Georgia, Lieutenant Vivian McFadden is sworn in as the first female African-American chaplain of the U.S. Navy.

1784

Death of "Mother" Ann Lee, English-born American religious leader and founder of United Society of Believers in Christ's Second Appearing, which came to be known as the Shakers.

1912

Young millionaire William W. Borden is ordained. Borden volunteered to serve with the China Inland Mission and went to Cairo to study Arabic in preparation for working with China's Muslim population. While in Egypt, however, he contracted cerebrospinal meningitis and died at age twenty-six in 1913.

1747

Birth of Thomas Coke, the first Methodist consecrated as a bishop to America. He served with Francis Asbury from 1784 to 1797 and later became president of the English Methodist Conference. Coke died at sea in 1814 while sailing to do missionary work in India.

1832

English Moravian hymn writer James Montgomery pens the words to "Holy, Holy, Holy Lord, God of Hosts." Montgomery is also remembered for authoring "The Lord Is My Shepherd," "Angels from the Realms of Glory," "Go to Dark Gethsemane," and "Prayer Is the Soul's Sincere Desire."

1898

Death of Alexander Crummell, African-American Episcopal clergyman, scholar, and missionary to West Africa. Ordained in 1844, Crummell served as president of Liberia College for twenty years.

1672

American Congregational clergyman
Solomon Stoddard is ordained as
pastor of the church in Northampton,
Massachusetts. He served in that single
pulpit for fifty-seven years, assisted
after 1727 by his grandson
Jonathan Edwards.

1069

Death of English prelate Aldred (Ealdred), archbishop of
York. On Christmas Day 1066, Aldred crowned William
the Conqueror king of England. Aldred was also the first
English bishop to make a pilgrimage to Jerusalem.

1928

The first international conference of
the Pocket Testament League convenes
in Birmingham, England.

1851

Birth of Francis E. Clark, Canadian-born
Congregational minister. In 1881 Clark founded the
Christian Endeavor movement, a forerunner and
prototype of today's church youth fellowships.

1845

The poem "Sweet Hour of Prayer" first appears in print in the *New York Observer*. It was written in 1842 by William W. Walford, a blind English lay preacher, and first set to music in 1861 by William B. Bradbury.

1771

English founder of Methodism, John Wesley, writes in a letter to a young Christian, "It is right to pour out our whole soul before Him that careth for us. But it is good, likewise, to unbosom ourselves to a friend, in whom we can confide."

1741

English composer George Frideric Handel finishes work on his great oratorio *Messiah*, which he composed in only twenty-four days.

1735

Birth of Robert Raikes, English newspaper editor, whose concern for the plight of boys in the local slums led him to experiment with opening a school to teach them reading and religion. The school met on Sundays, the one day of the week when the boys weren't working in the factories, and Raikes's success eventually led to the adoption of "Sunday schools" by churches worldwide.

1966

The American Bible Society
publishes its *Good News for Modern
Man* New Testament translation.

1870

Birth of Agnes Ozman, U.S. Pentecostal evangelist.
In 1901, while a student at Charles Parham's
Bethel Bible College in Topeka, Kansas, Miss Ozman
began speaking in tongues, and her experience
helped to ignite the modern Pentecostal revival.

1976

In Minneapolis the Episcopal Church
approves the ordination of women to
the priesthood, specifically approving
an action in which four bishops
had ordained eleven women to the
Episcopal priesthood on July 29, 1974—
at that time, in defiance of church law.

1924

Death of Anthony J. Showalter, American
Presbyterian hymn writer, best known for
composing the hymn tune "Showalter"
("Leaning on the Everlasting Arms").

1929

The Apostolic Orthodox Catholic Church is established in North America as an English-speaking, nonethnic, independent branch of the Russian Orthodox Church.

1787

Ratified on this date, Article 6, Section 3 of the U.S. Constitution reads, "No religious tests shall ever be required as a qualification to any office or public trust under the United States."

1924

Scottish-born American scholar James Moffatt completes his work on the Old Testament portion of what would become *A New Translation of the Bible, Containing the Old and New Testaments,* published in 1926.

1765

Birth of Oliver Holden, American carpenter and hymn composer. Holden's love for music led him to publish several hymnbooks and to compose the hymn tune "Coronation" ("All Hail the Power of Jesus' Name").

1772

Moravian missionaries complete construction of the first Protestant church west of the Alleghenies, in Schoenbrunn, Ohio. In 1773 the same missionaries built the first schoolhouse west of the Alleghenies. The Reverend David Zeisberger became the church's first preacher and the school's first teacher.

1740

During his second trip to America, English revivalist George Whitefield writes in his journal, "I saw regenerate souls among the Baptists, among the Presbyterians, among the Independents, and among the church folks—all children of God, and yet all born again in a different way."

1870

During the Franco-Prussian War,
Italian troops occupy Rome,
effectively ending the Vatican I
Ecumenical Council.

1900

Birth of Visser 't Hooft, Dutch Reformed ecumenical
leader, who served as secretary of the World Alliance of
YMCAs (1924–31), and later became founding general
secretary of the World Council of Churches (1948–66).

1522

Martin Luther publishes his German New Testament, based on Erasmus's 1516 Greek edition.

1452

Birth of Italian Dominican reformer Girolamo Savonarola. Preaching against licentiousness of the ruling class and the worldliness of the clergy, Savonarola led in the reformation of Florence. He was later excommunicated, arrested, condemned, and put to death for his attacks on Pope Alexander VI.

1734

The first Moravian settlement in America begins with the arrival of the Schwenkfelders (followers of reformer Caspar Schwenkfeld von Ossig) in Philadelphia.

1871

Death of Charlotte Elliott, Anglican hymn writer. Though an invalid during her last fifty years, Elliott authored 150 hymns, including "Just as I Am."

1642

Harvard College holds its first commencement exercises, conferring degrees on nine graduates. Founded in 1636 as Cambridge College, the school was renamed in 1638 in honor of the Reverend John Harvard, English clergyman and benefactor.

1747

Two weeks before dying from tuberculosis, colonial missionary to the American Indians David Brainerd pens in his journal, "Felt uncommonly peaceful; it seemed as if I had now done all my work in this world, and stood ready for my call to a better. As long as I see anything to be done for God, life is worth having; but O how vain and unworthy it is to live for any lower end!"

787

The Second Council of Nicaea opens—
the seventh of twenty-one ecumenical
councils recognized by the Catholic
Church. Under Pope Adrian I, the
council limited the veneration of icons
but condemned iconoclasm.

1939

Death of Juji Nakada, Japanese Christian evangelist,
who invited Charles and Lettie Cowman to Japan
in 1901. Under the Cowmans' inspiration, the
Oriental Missionary Society was established in 1910.

1800

Revival leaders Philip William Otterbein and Martin Boehm establish the Church of the United Brethren in Christ. Boehm was brought up in the Mennonite tradition, and Otterbein was a pastor of the German Reformed Church.

1866

Birth of Cleland B. McAfee, American Presbyterian clergyman, educator, and hymn writer. He taught systematic theology for eighteen years at McCormick Theological Seminary in Chicago, but he is best remembered for his hymn "There Is a Place of Quiet Rest."

1835

Eight churches in Florida establish the
Suwanee Association, the first official
Baptist organization in the state.

1651

Birth of Francis Daniel Pastorius, German Lutheran
emigration agent, who helped European Mennonites,
Pietists, and Quakers relocate to the American colony
of Pennsylvania. Pastorius was a central figure in the
establishment of Germantown, Pennsylvania.

1785

American Anglicans meet in Philadelphia to create a denomination independent from the Church of England. The new denomination came to be known as the Protestant Episcopal Church in the U.S.A.

1914

Birth of Catherine Marshall, American Presbyterian inspirational writer. The widow of U.S. Senate chaplain Peter Marshall, she authored *A Man Called Peter* (1951), following his premature death in 1949.

1931

C. S. Lewis undergoes a spiritual conversion while riding to the zoo in his brother Warren's motorcycle sidecar. Lewis later wrote, "When we set out, I did not believe that Jesus is the Son of God; and when we reached the zoo I did." Lewis's conversion followed a long conversation he'd had the week before with two Christian friends, J. R. R. Tolkien and Hugo Dyson.

929 or 935

Death of "good King" Wenceslas, Bohemian prince and martyr. During his reign (before he was murdered by his brother, Boleslaw), Wenceslas sought to care for the poor and to bring his people into closer connection with the Western world.

1979

Pope John Paul II becomes the
first Roman pontiff to visit Ireland.
More than 2.5 million of the country's
3.5 million Catholics saw the pope
during his three-day visit, which
crisscrossed the country.

1770

The day before his premature death at age fifty-six,
English revivalist George Whitefield prays, "Lord Jesus,
I am weary in thy work, but not of it."

1751

Phillip Doddridge, clergyman and author of the influential book *The Rise and Progress of Religion in the Soul*, sails from Falmouth for a warmer climate, in hopes of recovering from consumption. (He died a month later.)

420

Death of Jerome, Bible scholar and one of the most learned of the Latin Fathers. Originally from Rome, Jerome moved to Bethlehem, entered a monastery, and devoted himself to translating the Bible into Latin (bequeathing to the Western church the Vulgate Bible). He also prepared numerous works of ecclesiastical history and biblical interpretation.

1878

The Regions Beyond Mission, an evangelical Baptist organization, opens Harley College in Ireland. The school has since trained hundreds of missionaries.

1931

In a letter testifying to his recent religious conversion, British literary scholar C. S. Lewis writes, "I have just passed on from believing in God to definitely believing in Christ—in Christianity."

1930

The International Lutheran Hour debuts on a network of thirty-six American radio stations, with Dr. Walter A. Maier as speaker.

1846

Birth of Samuel R. Driver, English Semitic language scholar. Driver was Regius Professor of Hebrew at Oxford and coedited the *Hebrew-English Lexicon of the Old Testament* (1891–1905), known in scholarly circles as *Brown-Driver-Briggs*.

1852

In New York City the Reverend Thomas Gallaudet, an Episcopal priest, holds the first church service for deaf worshippers in a small chapel at New York University. Gallaudet held spoken worship services in the morning, and services using American Sign Language in the afternoon.

1690

Death of Robert Barclay, Scottish Quaker theologian. He published *An Apology for the True Christian's Divinity*, an important statement of Quaker doctrine.

1965

Pope Paul VI arrives in New York City, making him the first pope to visit America. On the first day of his visit, he celebrates Mass at Yankee Stadium and addresses the United Nations on the need for world peace.

1880

Birth of Homer A. Rodeheaver, American song evangelist and hymnbook publisher. An associate of Billy Sunday's for twenty years, Rodeheaver composed many gospel choruses and also established the Winona Lake Summer School of Music.

1744

David Brainerd begins missionary work among the Indians along New Jersey's Susquehanna River.

1703

Birth of Jonathan Edwards, considered by some the greatest theologian of American Puritanism. Edwards is widely remembered for his sermon "Sinners in the Hands of an Angry God," which he delivered in Enfield, Connecticut, in 1741.

1520

German reformer Martin Luther publishes his famous *Prelude on the Babylonian Captivity of the Church*, which attacks the sacramental system of the Catholic Church.

1816

Birth of William B. Bradbury, American music teacher, editor, and publisher. Bradbury composed the music for several popular hymns, including "He Leadeth Me," "Savior, Like a Shepherd Lead Us," "My Hope Is Built," and "Sweet Hour of Prayer."

1873

Baptist missionary Charlotte "Lottie" Moon arrives in China. Though born into wealth, Moon gave her whole life to missions and said, "If I had a thousand lives, I would give them all for the women of China."

1810

Birth of Henry Alford, Anglican clergyman and biblical philologist. He published a famous edition of the Greek New Testament (1849–61) and wrote the hymn "Come, Ye Thankful People, Come."

451

The Council of Chalcedon opens near Istanbul (Byzantium) in Asia Minor. Attended by more than five hundred bishops (the largest attendance of the early councils), the council produced a statement of faith, known afterward as the Chalcedonian Definition.

1927

Birth of Jim Elliot, American Plymouth Brethren missionary to Ecuador. In 1956, during an attempt to make contact with a hostile tribe, Jim and four fellow missionaries were killed by the very people they were attempting to evangelize. The story was published the following year by Elliot's widow, Elisabeth, in *Through Gates of Splendor*.

1976

Delegates to the American Lutheran Church convention in Washington DC agree to delete most references to gender in official church documents.

1974

Death of Czech-born German businessman Oskar Schindler, who is credited with saving more than two thousand Jews during the Holocaust. Although a strong Catholic, Schindler, at his own request, was buried in Jerusalem.

1821

Twenty-nine-year-old American law student Charles Finney is dramatically converted in the woods near his home. He immediately abandoned his law career and went on to become one of America's great revivalists, credited with the conversion of five hundred thousand souls.

1560

Birth of Dutch Reformed clergyman James (Jacob) Arminius. As a professor at Leiden (1603–09), Arminius could not accept the strict Calvinist teaching on predestination, and instead developed a doctrine of universal redemption and conditional predestination. Arminian theology is evident today in Methodist doctrine.

1998

Pope John Paul II decrees the first Jewish-born saint of the modern era, Edith Stein (1891–1942). A German Carmelite nun and spiritual writer, Stein was arrested by the Nazis because of her Jewish ancestry. She was murdered at Auschwitz on August 10, 1942.

1954

American Presbyterian missionary and apologist Francis Schaeffer writes in a letter, "Doctrinal rightness and rightness of ecclesiastical position are important, but only as a starting point to go on into a living relationship—and not as ends in themselves."

1762

The Association of Philadelphia Baptists votes to establish a college in Warren, Rhode Island. Incorporated in 1764 as Rhode Island College, the campus moved to Providence in 1770. In 1804 it became Brown University.

1895

Death of Cecil Frances Alexander, Irish poet, hymn writer, and wife of William Alexander, an Irish clergyman who became primate of Ireland in 1893. During her life, Alexander published several volumes of verse, and three of her poems later became popular hymns: "All Things Bright and Beautiful," "Jesus Calls Us," and "There Is a Green Hill Far Away."

1877

English devotional poet Frances Ridley Havergal pens the words to the hymn "Who Is on the Lord's Side?" based on 1 Chronicles 12:1–8.

1605

Death of Theodore Beza, John Calvin's successor in Geneva as the head of the Swiss Reformation.

1922

In Detroit the Evangelical Association
and the United Evangelical Church
merge to form the Evangelical Church,
with a combined membership
of 260,000.

1876

Birth of Henry A. (Harry) Ironside, Canadian-born
American clergyman and Bible teacher. Called the
"archbishop of Fundamentalism," Ironside pastored
Chicago's Moody Memorial Church from 1930 to 1948.

1932

Gladys Aylward sails from Liverpool, England, for Asia in an effort to bring the gospel to China. In 1958 her biography, *The Small Woman*, was made into an award-winning film: *Inn of the Sixth Happiness.*

1886

On the twenty-second anniversary of the death of his wife, Isabella, Scottish clergyman and biographer Andrew Bonar reflects in his diary, "I have learned...that the Lord can fill the soul with Himself, when He takes away what seemed indispensable to our happiness on earth."

1701

In Saybrook, Connecticut, the Reverend John Pierpont gains a charter to establish the Collegiate School under the auspices of a group of Congregationalists who were dissatisfied with the growing liberalism at Harvard. (The school later changed its name to Yale University.)

1812

Death of Henry Martyn, Anglican missionary to India and Persia. During his brief ministry, Martyn translated the New Testament into Urdu and Persian.

1979

The Nobel Peace Prize is awarded to
Mother Teresa (Agnes Bojaxhiu), the
Albanian Catholic nun who founded
the Society of the Missionaries
of Charity.

1912

Birth of Albino Luciani, Italian Catholic cardinal,
who became Pope John Paul I for thirty-four days,
before his death in 1978.

1469

Isabella of Castille marries Ferdinand II of Aragon, effectively uniting nearly all the Christian areas of Spain under one monarchy.

1595

Birth of Edward Winslow, English-born separatist and American Pilgrim leader. A passenger on the *Mayflower*, Winslow later served three terms as governor of the Plymouth Colony (1633, 1636, 1644).

1656

Massachusetts passes a law prohibiting
the further immigration of Quakers into
the Puritan colony. This prohibition led
indirectly to the later establishment of
the colony of Pennsylvania.

1720

Birth of John Woolman, American Quaker preacher
and abolitionist. In 1758 Woolman's inspired appeal
led the Philadelphia Yearly Meeting of Friends to
abandon and condemn slave holdings. Woolman's
Journal (first published in 1774) is recognized as
one of the classics of the inner life.

1870

With the outbreak of the Franco-Prussian War, the Vatican I Ecumenical Council in Rome ends before all the business at hand can be completed. When Italian troops took Rome, the council was suspended but never formally brought to a close.

1632

Birth of Christopher Wren, English church architect and astronomer, who proposed the plan for rebuilding London after the Great Fire of 1666. In all, Wren designed more than fifty London churches, including St. Paul's Cathedral.

1555

English Catholic Queen Mary Tudor begins a series of fierce persecutions against Protestantism, in which more than two hundred men, women, and children were put to death for their faith. Mary was startled to discover that the martyrdoms only intensified Protestant zeal.

1981

Dutch-born Catholic priest and educator Henri J. M. Nouwen notes in *Gracias: A Latin American Journal*, "A true spirituality cannot be constructed, built, or put together; it has to be recognized in the daily life of people who search together to do God's will in the world."

1746

An evangelical group within the Presbyterian Church establishes the College of New Jersey in Elizabethtown. The school moved to Princeton in 1752, and in 1896 changed its name to Princeton University.

1697

Birth of Katharina von Schlegel, German Lutheran sacred poet. One of her poems was translated into English by Jane L. Borthwick and became the hymn "Be Still, My Soul."

1819

Pioneer missionaries Hiram Bingham and Asa Thurston set sail, becoming the first Protestant missionaries to the Sandwich Islands (Hawaii). They were sponsored by the American Board of Commissioners for Foreign Missions.

1871

Birth of American New Testament scholar Edgar J. Goodspeed. He taught at the University of Chicago (1915–37), helped prepare the Revised Standard Version of the New Testament (1946), and coedited the renowned Smith and Goodspeed translation of the Bible (*The Complete Bible: An American Translation*).

1781

In Philadelphia, after a dispatch from General George Washington reporting his victory at Yorktown is read to Congress, the members adjourn to a nearby Dutch Lutheran church to offer up prayers of thanksgiving.

1826

Death of Ann (Hasseltine) Judson, American pioneer missionary. In 1812 she and Harriet Newell became the first two U.S. women commissioned to serve as overseas missionaries.

1941

The first Youth for Christ rally is held, at Bryant's Alliance Tabernacle in Manhattan.

1811

Birth of Carl F. W. Walther, who organized the Lutheran Church—Missouri Synod in the United States. He was also cofounder and president of Concordia Theological Seminary (1854–87) and authored *The Proper Distinction between Law and Gospel*.

312

Two days before the Battle of Milvian Bridge, Roman emperor Constantine has a vision of the cross of Christ. The vision ultimately turned him into a believer and a supporter of Christianity.

1822

Birth of Richard F. Weymouth, English Baptist philologist and New Testament scholar. His best-known work is *The New Testament in Modern Speech* (1903).

1771

Francis Asbury lands in Philadelphia to oversee America's few hundred Methodists. During his forty-five-year ministry in America, Asbury traveled an estimated three hundred thousand miles and delivered more than sixteen thousand sermons. By the time of his death in 1816, there were more than two hundred thousand Methodists in the United States.

1469

Birth of Desiderius Erasmus, Dutch Christian humanist, philosopher, and scholar. Regarded as the leader of the Renaissance in northern Europe, Erasmus's writings paved the way for the Reformation.

1871

At Ujiji, in modern Tanzania's Kigoma province, Henry Morton Stanley locates "missing" British missionary and explorer Dr. David Livingstone. Stanley's first words: "Dr. Livingstone, I presume?"

1949

Jim Elliot, American missionary and martyr, records in his journal, "He is no fool who gives what he cannot keep to gain that which he cannot lose."

1889

American clergyman Albert B. Simpson merges the Missionary Union (1883) and the Christian Alliance (1887) to form the Christian and Missionary Alliance, an ardent missions-centered denomination.

1885

Death of James Hannington, Anglican missionary prelate, who in 1884 was appointed as the first bishop of Eastern Equatorial Africa. Hannington was speared to death in Mombasa.

1976

Dr. Joseph H. Evans is elected president of the United Church of Christ, thereby becoming the first African-American leader of a predominantly white denomination.

1738

English founder of Methodism John Wesley explains in a letter, "By a 'Christian' I mean one who so believes in Christ as that sin hath no more dominion over him."

1517

German reformer Martin Luther nails his "Ninety-five Theses. . .for the Purpose of Eliciting Truth" to the door of the Wittenberg Palace Church. His action symbolically touches off what would grow to become the Protestant Reformation. By 1522 Protestant public worship was being celebrated in Wittenberg for the first time.

1896

Birth of Ethel Waters, African-American singer and actress. Waters was active in Billy Graham's evangelistic crusades during the 1950s and was known for singing "His Eye Is on the Sparrow."

1512

Italian Renaissance artist Michelangelo unveils his 5,808-square-foot masterpiece on the ceiling of the Sistine Chapel in the Vatican. He had been commissioned in 1508 by Pope Julius II to do a work depicting the story of the Bible.

1963

English linguistic scholar J. R. R. Tolkien summarizes Christian belief in a letter to his son: "In the last resort, faith is an act of will, inspired by love."

1917

British foreign secretary Arthur J. Balfour issues the Balfour Declaration, calling for "establishment in Palestine of a national home for the Jewish people." This document plants a seed that led to the founding of the modern state of Israel in 1948.

1773

Birth of Stephen Grellet, French Quaker clergyman, missionary, and philanthropist. Traveling through Europe and North America, Grellet reported on conditions in prisons and poorhouses, and introduced reformer Elizabeth Fry to her life's work among prisoners.

1818

Pliny Fisk sets sail for Palestine. Ordained by the American Board of Commissioners for Foreign Missions, Fisk was the first American missionary to travel to the Near East.

1759

Martin Luther's male lineage ends with the death of his great-great-grandson, Martin Gottlob Luther, a Dresden attorney.

1646

The Massachusetts Bay Colony passed a law making it a capital offense to deny that the Bible was the Word of God. A person convicted of the offense was liable to the death penalty.

1903

Birth of (Henry) Watchman Nee, Chinese spiritual leader. Converted in 1920, Nee adopted the Plymouth Brethren doctrine of the victorious life and founded an Evangelical Christian group known as the Little Flock. Nee authored several devotional classics, including *Sit, Walk, Stand* (1958) and *The Normal Christian Life* (1961). Imprisoned by the Chinese government in 1952, Watchman Nee spent his last twenty years in prison.

1935

In Nashville the Cooperative General
Association of Free Will Baptists
(northern United States) and the
General Conference of Free Will
Baptists (southern United States)
merge to form the National Association
of Free Will Baptists.

1841

Birth of Daniel C. Roberts, American clergyman and
hymn writer. Roberts's name endures as author of the
hymn "God of Our Fathers, Whose Almighty Hand."

1789

In Baltimore the first American Catholic diocese is created by Pope Pius VI in the newly independent United States of America. Father John Carroll, is appointed as the first American Roman Catholic bishop.

1935

Death of American revivalist William Ashley "Billy" Sunday. After a professional baseball career from 1883 to 1890, Sunday was ordained as a Presbyterian minister in 1903. Until the advent of Billy Graham, no other American evangelist preached to as many people nor counted as many conversions as did Billy Sunday.

1637

Controversial colonial American religious leader Anne Hutchinson is convicted of heresy and banished from the Massachusetts Bay Colony. Mrs. Hutchinson moved to Rhode Island with her family and friends.

1918

Birth of American Baptist evangelist William Franklin "Billy" Graham. Converted at sixteen under revivalist Mordecai Ham, Graham began an evangelistic career in 1944 with Youth for Christ. In 1950 he founded the Billy Graham Evangelistic Association and went on to conduct evangelistic crusades all over the world. During his meetings, more than two million individuals have come forward to accept Christ.

1837

Mt. Holyoke Seminary opens in Massachusetts. Founded by Mary Lyon, it was the first college in the United States established specifically for the education of women.

1931

Newly converted to the Christian faith, British literary scholar C. S. Lewis writes in a letter, "One needs the sweetness to start one on the spiritual life, but once started, one must learn to obey God for his own sake, not for the pleasure."

1732

In Scala, Italy, St. Alfonso Maria de Liguori establishes the Congregation of the Most Holy Redeemer (Redemptorists). The religious order was officially approved in 1749.

1799

Birth of Asa Mahan, American educator and Congregational clergyman. As the first president of Oberlin College in Ohio (1835–50), Mahan was instrumental in establishing interracial education and the granting of college degrees to women.

432

Patrick, a young British monk who had once been held captive by the Irish, returns to the land of his captivity and begins a lifelong mission to the Irish people. Ministering there for more than fifty years, St. Patrick came to be known as the "apostle of Ireland."

1483

Birth of Martin Luther, German reformer. His "Ninety-five Theses," posted on the door of the Wittenberg Palace Church in 1517 inaugurated the Protestant Reformation in Europe. Luther also translated the Bible into German and authored thirty-seven hymns, including "A Mighty Fortress."

1620

The Mayflower Compact is signed by the forty-one English separatists among the 101 passengers aboard the *Mayflower*. The document serves as the basis for organizing the Pilgrims into "a civil body politic." Democratic in form, the Compact comprised the first written American constitution and remained in force until 1691.

1561

Death of Hans Tausen, advocate of the Danish Reformation. Known as the "Danish Luther," Tausen served as Protestant bishop in Ribe (1542–61) and translated the Pentateuch into Danish.

1899

American evangelist Dwight L. Moody begins his last evangelistic campaign in Kansas City, Missouri. Becoming ill during the final service, Moody was unable to complete his message. He died on December 22.

1556

Dutch Anabaptist reformer Menno Simons writes in a letter, "I can neither teach nor live by the faith of others. I must live by my own faith as the Spirit of the Lord has taught me through His Word."

1564

Pope Pius IV orders his bishops and scholars to subscribe to "Professio fidei," the profession of the tridentine faith formulated at the Council of Trent (1545–63) as the new and final definition of the Roman Catholic faith.

1913

Birth of Alexander Scourby, American actor. His most memorable screen role was in *Giant* (1956), but he became better known for his resonant bass voice, which he loaned to some of the first readings of the King James Bible on audiocassette.

1941

Inter-Varsity Christian Fellowship
is incorporated in Chicago.
An interdenominational youth
organization with chapters established
at both colleges and schools of nursing,
IVCF provides Christian fellowship,
nurture, and discipleship among
Christian college students.

1864

Birth of Helen H. Lemmel, English-born sacred
vocalist and hymn writer. She penned five hundred
hymns (many for children), including the still-popular
"Turn Your Eyes upon Jesus."

1626

The English separatists known to history as the *Mayflower* Pilgrims, having lived in their American colony for six years, buy out their London investors for £1,800—the equivalent of $300,000 in today's dollars.

1917

Death of Oswald Chambers, Scottish Bible teacher and author. During the last years of his life, Chambers served as a chaplain to British troops stationed in Egypt during World War I. His posthumous devotional, *My Utmost for His Highest*, has become a classic.

1946

The Church of the United Brethren in Christ and the Evangelical Church merge to form the Evangelical United Brethren Church, in Johnstown, Pennsylvania.

1828

Birth of Timothy Dwight, American Congregational clergyman. Dwight was a renowned New Testament scholar and served on the revision committee of the American Standard Version of the Bible.

1758

English churchman Philip Embury marries Margaret Switzer. After emigrating to America, Embury was encouraged by his cousin, Barbara Heck, to establish a Methodist society in New York City (1768). Embury thus became the first Methodist preacher in North America.

1808

Death of David Zeisberger, Moravian missionary to Native Americans. He established Indian congregations in Pennsylvania, Ohio, and Canada, but the churches he founded did not survive.

1866

English devotional writer Katherine Hankey pens the verses we sing today as the hymn "I Love to Tell the Story."

1800

Birth of John Nelson Darby, Irish-born English spiritual reformer. Darby was a gifted exponent of the early Plymouth Brethren movement. Following a schism that began in 1845, Darby became the leader of the stricter Exclusive Brethren.

1910

Swedish Pentecostal missionaries Daniel Berg and Adolf Vingren arrive in Brazil. In 1918 they established the first Pentecostal church in Brazil, which grew into the country's largest Protestant body, the Assemblies of God.

1672

Richard Baxter, preaching illegally in his own home after a ten-year silence, says, "I preached as never sure to preach again, and as a dying man to dying men."

1850

Frances Jane "Fanny" Crosby, blind from the age of six months, undergoes a dramatic spiritual conversion at age thirty. Fifteen years later she began writing the first of more than eight thousand devotional verses. Many of these remain popular today as hymns, including "Blessed Assurance," "All the Way My Savior Leads Me," "Rescue the Perishing," and "Jesus, Keep Me Near the Cross."

1741

Birth of Samuel Kirkland, American missionary to the Oneida Indians. Kirkland was influential in keeping the Six Nations neutral during the American Revolution. He also was the founder of the Hamilton Oneida Academy (1793), which later became Hamilton College.

1948

The Sunday morning religious program
Lamp unto My Feet debuts on CBS
television. It becomes one of TV's
longest-running network shows,
airing through January 1979.

1907

Birth of James Alonzo "Jim" Bishop, American
journalist, syndicated newspaper columnist, and editor
of *Catholic Digest*. Bishop gave new life to great moments
in history through his "day" books, including
his 1957 chronicle *The Day Christ Died*.

1633

Irish Catholic Cecilius Calvert (Lord Calvert) sends two ships (the *Ark* and the *Dove*) from Ireland to establish a colony in America as a refuge for Catholics. Calvert's work earned him the nickname "Colonizer of Maryland."

1963

Death of C. S. Lewis, English literary scholar, novelist, critic, and Christian apologist. Well known for authoring The Chronicles of Narnia (1950–56), Lewis also wrote other Christian classics, including *The Screwtape Letters* (1942), *The Great Divorce* (1945), *Miracles* (1947), and *Mere Christianity* (1952).

1947

Eliezer L. Sukenik of Jerusalem's Hebrew University receives word of the existence of the Dead Sea Scrolls. The ancient documents (ca. 200 BC–AD 70) had been discovered the previous winter by two Bedouin shepherds in the vicinity of Qumran.

1906

Death of Wilhelm Wrede, German Lutheran New Testament scholar. He was named in the title of Albert Schweitzer's classic christological study, *The Quest for the Historical Jesus: From Reimarus to Wrede.*

1880

In Montgomery, Alabama, more than 150 delegates from Baptist churches in eleven states meet to form the Baptist Foreign Missions Convention of the United States. The Reverend William H. McAlpine is elected as the organization's first president.

1713

Birth of Junipero Serra, Spanish-born Franciscan missionary to western North America. Serra arrived in Mexico in 1749, extended his labors to northern California in 1769, and established nine of the first twenty-one Franciscan missions founded along the Pacific coast, including San Francisco, Santa Barbara, Santa Clara, and San Juan Capistrano. Serra has been aptly called the "apostle of California."

2348 BC

According to the reckoning of Irish archbishop James Ussher, the "Great Deluge" (Noah's flood) began on this date. Ussher's *Chronology of the Old and New Testaments* is the source of the dates inserted in the margins of many editions of the King James Version of the Bible.

1787

Birth of Franz Gruber, Austrian Catholic musician and choral director. Gruber wrote more than ninety musical compositions yet is remembered today for a single hymn tune, written for his pastor, Joseph Mohr, on Christmas Eve in 1818: "Stille Nacht" ("Silent Night").

1789

President George Washington
proclaims this date (a Thursday) as the
first national Thanksgiving Day holiday.
In 1863 President Abraham Lincoln
established the fourth Thursday in
November as a permanent annual
Thanksgiving Day.

1858

Birth of Katherine Drexel, American Catholic missionary
and founder of the Sisters of the Blessed Sacrament
for Indians and Colored People. In 1915 she founded
Xavier University in New Orleans.

1921

The first church of the airwaves
is established when services of the
Radio Church of America are broadcast
by Walter J. Garvey from his home
in the Bronx.

1862

Birth of Adelaide Pollard, American Presbyterian
hymn writer and mystic. Of the several hymns she
penned, "Have Thine Own Way, Lord"
is perhaps the most popular.

1950

The National Council of the Churches of Christ in the United States of America is established in Cleveland, Ohio, by a constitutional convention comprising fourteen Protestant, Anglican, and Eastern Orthodox denominations. Today the NCCC serves to administer disaster relief, strengthen family life, provide leadership training, and promote world peace.

1918

Birth of Madeleine L'Engle, American author, who won the 1963 Newbery Medal for *A Wrinkle in Time*.

1970

In Nagpur, India, six church entities—
the Anglicans, the United Church
of Northern India, the Baptists,
the Methodists, the Church of the
Brethren, and the Disciples of Christ—
merge to form the Church of India.

1847

Marcus Whitman, American Presbyterian medical
missionary to the American Northwest Indians, is
murdered by a party of Cayuse Indians in present-day
Washington State. Along with Whitman, his wife,
Narcissa, and twelve others were also massacred.

1894

In Naperville, Illinois, seven groups
withdraw from the Evangelical
Association to form the United
Evangelical Church.

1725

Birth of Martin Boehm, American church founder and
Mennonite bishop. Boehm was later excluded from the
Mennonite communion for associating with persons of
other sects. In 1789 he joined with German Reformed
pastor Philip Otterbein to establish the Church of the
United Brethren in Christ.

1917

Edward J. Flanagan establishes Boys Town, a home for orphaned and problem children in Omaha, Nebraska. Father Flanagan believed there was no such thing as a boy beyond hope.

1867

Death of Philaret (Vasily Mikhailovich Drozdov), Russian prelate and writer. As Metropolitan of Moscow (1825–67), he composed a standard catechism (1829), which was adopted by the Holy Synod of the Church of Russia.

1960

The archbishop of Canterbury, Geoffrey Fisher, meets with Pope John XXIII in the Vatican. It is the first meeting between leaders of the Anglican and Roman Catholic faiths since the founding of the Church of England in 1534.

1831

Birth of Francis Nathan Peloubet, American Congregational clergyman, Bible commentator, and author of Sunday school literature. Peloubet published forty-four annual volumes of his *Select Notes on the International Sunday School Lessons*.

1976

The Association of Evangelical Lutheran Churches (AELC) is formally organized at a two-day meeting in Chicago. Membership is largely drawn from former affiliates of the Lutheran Church—Missouri Synod, as well as several other independent Lutheran congregations.

1902

Birth of Mitsuo Fuchida, the general who flew the lead plane in the Japanese attack on Pearl Harbor. Following World War II, General Fuchida was converted from Buddhism to Christianity by representatives of the Pocket Testament League.

1893

The first three missionaries of the Sudan Interior Mission arrive in Nigeria. Of the three, Walter Gowans and Thomas Kent died of fever within a year. The third man, Rowland Bingham, returned home in broken health but nevertheless served as general director of SIM until his death in 1942.

1985

Dutch-born Catholic priest and educator Henri J. M. Nouwen reflects in *The Road to Daybreak*, "The heart knows so much more than the mind."

1948

On WPIX-TV in New York City, the first televised church service in sign language is conducted by the Reverend Floyd F. Possehl, who reads the scriptures and preaches from St. Matthew's Lutheran Church for the Deaf, in Queens.

1907

Death of Priscilla Jane Owens, American Methodist schoolteacher and hymn writer. Her best-known hymns are "Jesus Saves" and "We Have an Anchor."

1787

Cokesbury College, the first Methodist college in America, opens in Abingdon, Maryland. It was named after bishops Thomas Coke and Francis Asbury.

1821

Birth of Dora Greenwell, English devotional author, who is best remembered as the author of the hymn "I Am Not Skilled to Understand."

1941

The popular wartime phrase, "Praise the Lord and pass the ammunition!" is coined by naval chaplain Howell M. Forgy aboard the cruiser U.S.S. *New Orleans*, which was among the ships attacked during the Japanese air raid on Pearl Harbor.

521

Birth of Columba, Irish Celtic priest and "apostle to Scotland." In 563 Columba left his native Ireland, set up a monastery on the Scottish island of Iona, and from there sent missionaries to modern-day Holland, France, Switzerland, Germany, and Italy. Columba later made forays into Scotland, where the Picts, a tribe of pagans, were won to the faith.

1630

Roger Williams sails for America to escape persecution in England for preaching against church-state unions. Persecuted also in the New World, he later fled to Narragansett Bay, where he founded a settlement named Providence. There Williams established the colony of Rhode Island and founded the first Baptist church in America.

1691

Death of Richard Baxter, English pastor and theologian. Considered the greatest Puritan preacher of his day, Baxter's theology portrayed Christ's death as an act of universal redemption, penal and vicarious, though not strictly substitutionary. Baxter's writings include *The Saints' Everlasting Rest* (1650).

1917

The Ottoman Empire surrenders Jerusalem to the British, ending seven hundred years of rule by Muslim Turks. Palestine remained a protectorate of Great Britain until Israel became an independent state in 1948.

1608

Birth of John Milton, English Puritan poet and essayist. Milton wrote in four languages but is best remembered today for his metrical epic masterpieces, *Paradise Lost* (1667) and *Paradise Regained* (1671), both of which were written after he lost his eyesight in 1652.

1948

The United Nations General Assembly adopts a "Universal Declaration of Human Rights," which includes the following article: "Everyone has the right to freedom of thought, conscience, and religion. . .and freedom. . .to manifest his religion or belief in teaching, practice, worship, and observance."

1739

English revivalist George Whitefield prays, "Lord, grant we may always keep between the two extremes of distrusting or tempting Thee."

1518

Swiss reformer Ulrich Zwingli is elected "people's priest" at Old Minster, the principal church in Zurich, where he served for the remaining thirteen years of his life.

1792

Birth of Joseph Mohr, German Catholic priest and author of the Christmas poem "Stille Nacht" ("Silent Night"), which was set to music by church organist Franz Gruber.

1682

The Great Law of the Colony of Pennsylvania is passed. Quaker founder William Penn wrote into this law the principle of religious tolerance, no doubt inspired by the persecution he and his fellow Quakers had suffered in England and America.

1840

Birth of Charlotte "Lottie" Moon, American missionary appointed by the Southern Baptist Mission Board to serve in P'ing-tu, China. Today Lottie Moon is regarded as the patron saint of Southern Baptist missions.

1930

Igor Stravinsky's *Symphony of Psalms*, a work for chorus and orchestra, is first performed in Brussels. The piece is a setting of the Latin Vulgate translation of Psalms 39, 40, and 150. Stravinsky believed that "the principal virtue of music is [as] a means of communication with God."

1985

Dutch-born Catholic priest and educator Henri J. M. Nouwen reflects in *The Road to Daybreak*, "I must pray for the strength and courage to be truly obedient to Jesus, even if he calls me to go where I would rather not go."

1853

Illinois Institute opens under the Wesleyans. In 1860 the financially troubled institution requested help from the wealthier Congregationalists. Jonathan Blanchard, a Presbyterian pastor and academic, was appointed president, and the school changed its name to Wheaton College.

1836

Birth of Frances Ridley Havergal, English devotional poet. An incessant writer, she penned a number of enduring hymns, including "Take My Life and Let It Be," "Lord, Speak to Me That I May Speak," and "Who Is on the Lord's Side?"

1870

African-American leader Robert Payne organizes the Colored Methodist Episcopal Church in Jackson, Mississippi. The first two elected CME bishops are W. H. Miles and R. H. Vanderhorst.

1843

Birth of Albert B. Simpson, Canadian-born American clergyman and hymn writer. Ordained in the Presbyterian Church, Simpson later founded the Christian and Missionary Alliance. In 1883 he established Nyack College, North America's earliest surviving Bible and missionary training college.

1904

Fifteen-year-old (Sadhu) Sundar Singh burns a Bible in his rage at the death of his mother. A few days later, he was miraculously converted to the Christian faith, and went on to become an apostle to India and Tibet.

1714

Birth of George Whitefield, English revivalist. Associated with the Wesley brothers during his university years, Whitefield embarked on a lifelong calling as an evangelist. He died in Newburyport, Massachusetts, during his seventh visit to the American colonies.

1889

American revivalist Dwight L. Moody establishes the Bible Institute for Home and Foreign Missions in Chicago. Raised a Unitarian in Massachusetts, Moody converted to evangelical Christianity. In 1856 he left his work as a shoe salesman in Boston to engage in "home missionary" work in Chicago.

1807

Birth of John Greenleaf Whittier, American Quaker poet. Whittier used his pen to raise the conscience of the North against slavery. "Ichabod" was among the best of his poems. He is also remembered for authoring the hymn "Dear Lord and Father of Mankind."

1904

Indian mystic Sundar Singh is converted to Christianity. He later donned the robe of a Sadhu (Hindu holy man) in an endeavor to present Christianity in a Hindu form. Singh disappeared in April 1929 while undertaking a strenuous mission in Tibet.

1707

Birth of Charles Wesley, English hymn writer and younger brother of John Wesley. "As the "poet of Methodism," Charles penned sixty-five hundred hymns, including "And Can It Be That I Should Gain," "Jesus, Lover of My Soul," "Hark! The Herald Angels Sing," and "Love Divine, All Loves Excelling."

1861

Charles Haddon Spurgeon, English Baptist preacher, erects an almshouse for the elderly. Spurgeon later established a school for needy children in London (1864), founded the Stockwell Orphanages (1866), and established a private hospital (1867).

1808

Birth of Horatius Bonar, Scottish clergyman and hymnist, known as the greatest hymn writer among the Scots. Bonar prepared three series of *Hymns of Faith and Hope*, including such favorites as "Here, O My Lord, I See Thee Face to Face" and "I Heard the Voice of Jesus Say."

1787

Under the guidance of their third leader, the Reverend Joseph Meacham, the Shakers in America begin experiencing revival.

1934

Death of Adelaide A. Pollard, American Presbyterian ascetic, mystic, and hymn writer. She is best remembered as the author of the hymn "Have Thine Own Way Lord."

1849

"Shepherd of Tender Youth," the earliest known hymn in Christendom (outside the New Testament), first appears in print in English in *The Congregationalist*, a denominational magazine edited by the poem's translator, the Reverend Henry Martyn Dexter. The original hymn was authored by Clement of Alexandria (ca. 170–220).

1795

Birth of Robert Moffat, Scottish Congregational missionary to Africa. Sent by the London Missionary Society in 1816, Moffat spent forty-nine years in the field, where he translated the Bible and developed a major missionary community. In 1839 Moffat visited England and persuaded David Livingstone to join him in Africa.

1838

John and Hannah Hunt arrive in the Fiji islands as English Methodist missionaries. At that time cannibalism ravaged the islands of Rewa, Somosomo, Lakemba, and Viwa. John soon translated the New Testament into Fijian, and by the time of his death in 1848, much of Fiji had been transformed by the Hunts' evangelistic work.

1763

John Wesley writes in his journal, "Lord, let me not live to be useless!"

1531

Swiss reformer Heinrich Bullinger takes the place of the slain Ulrich Zwingli as pastor of the Grossmunster Church of Zurich. Bullinger continues Zwingli's practice of preaching through the Bible verse by verse, and his wisdom and influence soon spread across Europe.

1830

Birth of Charlotte A. (Pye) Barnard, English poet and balladeer. One of the more prolific ballad writers of the nineteenth century, Barnard composed the hymn tune "Barnard" ("Give of Your Best to the Master").

1818

The first singing of "Silent Night" ("Stille Nacht") is heard. The original German verses of this timeless Christmas carol were written by Joseph Mohr, parish priest of Oberndorf, Austria. Its music was composed by church organist Franz Gruber.

1912

Death of Charlotte "Lottie" Moon, American Baptist missionary to China. After forty years of service with the Southern Baptist Mission Board, Moon suffered with the Chinese people in a terrible famine. Slowly starving while sharing her food with others, she later died aboard the ship that was taking her back to America.

336

The earliest reference to observing Jesus' nativity on December 25 is found in the Philocalian calendar of 354, which dates the Roman origin of the practice to 336.

1413

In a letter composed nineteen months before he was burned at the stake, Bohemian reformer Jan Hus proclaims, "Rejoice that the immortal God is born so that mortal men may live in eternity."

1790

In Philadelphia the First Day Society adopts a constitution, the purpose of which is to instruct the rising generation from the text of the Bible and "from such other moral and religious books as the society might, from time to time, direct."

1887

Birth of Charles B. Booth, American social reformer and grandson of Salvation Army founder William Booth. Charles served as head of the Volunteers of America from 1949 to 1958.

1943

The film *Song of Bernadette* is released by the Fox Film Corporation (later Twentieth Century Fox). The film tells the story of Bernadette Soubirous, a fourteen-year-old French Catholic peasant girl who experienced eighteen visions of the Virgin Mary at Lourdes in 1858.

1893

Birth of Samuel M. Shoemaker, American Episcopal clergyman, whose work extended into missions, radio broadcasting, and a ministry to university students. Shoemaker also assisted the founders of Alcoholics Anonymous in formulating their Twelve Steps.

1384

English reformer John Wycliffe, "morning star of the Reformation," suffers a paralyzing stroke. He died three days later, on his sixty-fourth birthday. Wycliffe authored the first complete translation of the Bible into English. His life also influenced other reformers, including Jan Hus, Martin Luther, and John Calvin.

1741

English revivalist George Whitefield advises in a letter, "Go to bed seasonably, and rise early. Redeem your precious time...that not one moment of it may be lost. Be much in secret prayer. Converse less with man, and more with God."

1851

The first American branch of the Young Men's Christian Association (YMCA) opens in Boston. Englishman George Williams founded the movement in London in 1844 when he began holding meetings with his fellow workers for Bible study and prayer.

1170

Thomas à Becket, archbishop of Canterbury from 1162, is murdered by four of King Henry II's Norman knights. Once a close friend of Henry's, as his archbishop, Becket had opposed the king over several critical tax and church issues.

1927

The International Church of the Foursquare Gospel is incorporated in Los Angeles. Founded in 1923 by evangelist Aimee Semple McPherson, the denomination provided a significant outlet for women in ministry. Today more than 40 percent of its ministerial roles are filled by women.

1678

Birth of William Croft, English organist. Early in life he wrote secular music. Later he became one of England's most significant composers of church music. Today Croft is best remembered for the hymn tune "St. Anne" ("O God, Our Help in Ages Past").

999

European Christians expect the
world to end after this night—
the last day before AD 1000.

1977

Russian Orthodox liturgical scholar Alexander
Schmemann reflects in his journal, "As the sacrament is
impossible without bread, wine, and water, so religion
requires peace, true daily peace. Without it, religion
becomes a neurosis, a self-deception, a delusion."

Name Index